Cave bureau

LOUISIANA MUSEUM OF MODERN ART
LARS MÜLLER PUBLISHERS

Supported by Realdania
Sponsor of architectural exhibitions
at Louisiana Museum of Modern Art

Cave bureau

Texts by
Kabage Karanja and Stella Mutegi
András Szántó
Mark Williams, Jan Zalasiewicz and Molly Desorgher
Kathryn Yusoff
Joy Mboya
Ngaire Blankenberg
Lesley Lokko

Foreword

Cave_bureau – The Anthropocene Museum is the sixth and final exhibition in the series *The Architect's Studio*, held at Louisiana Museum of Modern Art since 2017. Throughout the series visitors have been able to acquaint themselves with international architects who are challenging the field at its core.

The various design studios have brought with them not only other methods, but also other parameters for good architecture. Over the years, this has opened up a discussion not only about where building culture is heading, but also what architects are able to work with, and how. For instance, the most recent exhibition with the London-based research unit Forensic Architecture made it clear that through aesthetic analysis and visualisations of space, architects are able to make contributions to spheres beyond building culture. By presenting existing spaces through drawings, models and animations, Forensic Architecture makes it possible to visualise events that have taken place within architecture – and by exposing spaces, crimes against people are also exposed. It became obvious that architecture, materials and landscape – that is, planning – is always cultural and political. For the last exhibition in the series, it was therefore natural for us to invite a studio that also works to reveal the societal and cultural structures and patterns that coexist with the ways we manage spaces. Under the title The Anthropocene Museum, Kenyan Cave_bureau works to formulate a new architecture in which its prior analysis and research opens up discussion about what lies outside the practice, but which we still call space: resonant space, experiential space, space for reflection.

Under its founders, Kabage Karanja and Stella Mutegi, Cave_bureau works to describe our common time from an African perspective, keeping in mind the continent's vital role in the green shift. In their eyes the architecture of the future must rely on knowledge of geology and connection to nature, as it traditionally has done in Africa. The architecture through which we have built our society in modern times and the way we view space, borders, cities and collective ties have to be reassessed by taking a critical stance towards anthropocentrism. The jumping-off point for The Anthropocene Museum is the term for the geological epoch in which we may already be living, namely the Anthropocene. The Earth's geological periods are determined on the basis of significant changes in the soil column and since the actions, inventions and the progress of humanity are believed to be driving the changes to the Earth's environment, the Anthropocene (*antropos* = human, *cene* or *kainos* = new) is now being proposed as a new geological epoch to follow the Holocene, which has lasted since the end of the last ice age, 11,700 years ago. There is still debate as to when, if at all, this period began: with industrialisation, with the great acceleration after World War II, or perhaps as early as the agricultural revolution. Humanity has been instrumental in changing the Earth in just a few thousand years, changes in both landscape and climate which we can see with our own eyes.

The Anthropocene is a fact of life we are reminded of every day. The criticism, however, is in part that it is too early to understand the significance of these changes, and in part that the term 'Anthropocene' affords human beings greater power and importance than we perhaps possess. Regardless of objective measurements, geology – and every other science – is conveyed on the basis of a given mode of thinking, and thus a language. The Anthropocene was given its name by Western scientists who see humanity, not nature or other species, as the key player. When Japanese geologists discovered the same changes in the soil column, they did not refer to this new era as the 'epoch of humanity'; rather, the changes were perceived as an interplay between three elements – biosphere, geosphere and humanosphere – with roots in the idea of *shinra bansho*, which can be translated as 'all things in the universe.'[1] The same scientific measurements were thus being described from a different, more holistic way of thinking. Perhaps the anthropocentric worldview, which has elevated man above nature, is what has created problems for the planet in the first place. A number of proposals for naming the epoch are doing the rounds: Capitalocene, Thermocene or Plantationocene, with the latter referencing plantations, and thus also colonialism, where redistribution of property and labour result in increased energy emissions and – over time – in changes in the soil layer. Although – and because – none of the concepts are perfect, we need them all. More than anything else, the Anthropocene is perhaps the first opportunity to bring the natural sciences and the humanities together around a concept that is equally real to both sciences. The environmental crisis and the crisis of human identity meet here and are mutually dependent. As Cave_bureau points out, architects have the opportunity to step in and create space for this meeting.

The point of departure for Cave_bureau's work is spaces that are millions of years old; they analyse and stage those spaces to rethink the architectural discourse. When Cave_bureau turned back to the caves at Mount Suswa in Kenya, they were struck by the similarity with architectural masterpieces, such as the Pantheon in Rome. The architecture of the caves, and the fact that our early ancestors very likely saw the same spaces and perhaps formed the very first ideas about architecture, set in motion thoughts about the treasures that go unrecorded in the history of architecture and about the coexistence of architecture and nature. When Cave_bureau sets out to tell the story of their own people and devise architectural healing projects based on the caves, it is about the right of the continent to imagine its own future – to rewind in order to return with the appropriate knowledge for our common now.

Although they are fantastic areas of wilderness where baboons, giant bats and leopards live, the caves also harbour stories of some of the very first hominids – our common ancestors – and the recent history that has shaped Africa and the continent's peoples, including the history of slavery in East Africa: enslaved people were crammed together in the caves before their departure overseas. Later, the caves were the setting for Kenyan freedom fighters who rebelled against the British colonialists and sought refuge in the underground cave systems. European colonial powers seized the land and reallocated it by drawing lines with a ruler – ignoring nature and the existence of the original nomadic peoples who lived there. In Kenya and across Africa in general, there is therefore a void between the building culture of Indigenous cultures and the urban planning of the West, where growth has leapfrogged nature. This situation has not been given much space in the history of architecture, while at the same time the number of African architects who design and build in Africa remains small in comparison to the continent's size and population. If as a society we are to solve the enormous challenge presaged by the Anthropocene, we must not retrace the patterns of colonialism today, when the wholesale extraction of geothermal energy from African land is being planned with no regard for the landscape, wildlife and Indigenous people.[2] You might say that decarbonisation and decolonisation are two sides of the same coin.

Cave_bureau's architectural projects are gentle interventions in the landscape that support Indigenous people and the rhythms of nature intended to relate to a modern Africa and heal fissures in the culture. Inspired by the impressive spaces of the caves, they create solutions to some of Kenya's most pressing problems: The *Cow Corridor* seeks to re-establish the Maasai grazing routes through the capital Nairobi, which has been forbidden territory for cows since the British partition of the country. With The Anthropocene Museum as the overarching title for all its projects, Cave_bureau links architecture with the ongoing discussion around our relationship with the past, and how the past is appropriated in the present and for the future. The Anthropocene Museum will not be built, but will *take place* as a continuous and lively discussion. It is not a building, but a project that appears at different exhibitions and fora where the Anthropocene is being discussed. It is a movement that shares knowledge. It reassesses the role of the architect, societies and even the geochronological epochs that are made possible by our spatial understanding of the world.

A big, warm thank you to Kabage Karanja and Stella Mutegi for a rewarding collaboration on the exhibition and this catalogue. Thanks to Noelle Oyunga and everyone at Cave_bureau. Thanks to Lesley Lokko; Mark Williams, Jan Zalasiewicz and Molly Desorgher; Kathryn Yussof; Joy Mboya; Ngaire Blankenberg; and András Szántó, all of whom contributed their knowledge and engagement to the texts in this catalogue. Thank you to Center for Information Technology and Architecture at the Royal Danish Academy's School of Architecture, where Phil Ayres, Mette Ramsgaard Thomsen and Jack Young's research into kagome weaving and their generous commitment have made it possible to turn Cave_bureau's ideas into an exhibition. Thanks to Sabine Kongsted, Chloe Liang and Sebastian Hedevang for dedicated weaving. Last but not least, we would like to express our appreciation to Realdania for their ongoing support for the exhibition series *The Architect's Studio*. Being on or navigating at the edge of disciplines for this series can be more than a communication challenge to a fruitful relationship between an institution and its supporters and sponsors – however, Realdania has, once again in our mutual history, shown both dedication to and faith in the projects that Louisiana has proposed. We are very grateful for this kind of ideal relation. The exhibitions have confirmed Louisiana's role as an international communicator of architecture. It is our pleasure to add to the growing awareness of humanity's place in the world, our forms of living together, our dreams and visions. We have been delighted to work on this with Realdania, as our long-standing partnership continues to grow.

Poul Erik Tøjner
Director, Louisiana Museum of Modern Art

Kjeld Kjeldsen
Curator

Mette Marie Kallehauge
Curator

Notes

1   https://www.tandfonline.com/doi/full/10.1080/00141844.2015.1105838.
2   https://www.theelephant.info/features/2020/12/04/geothermal-development-in-kenya-the-good-the-bad-and-the-ugly/.

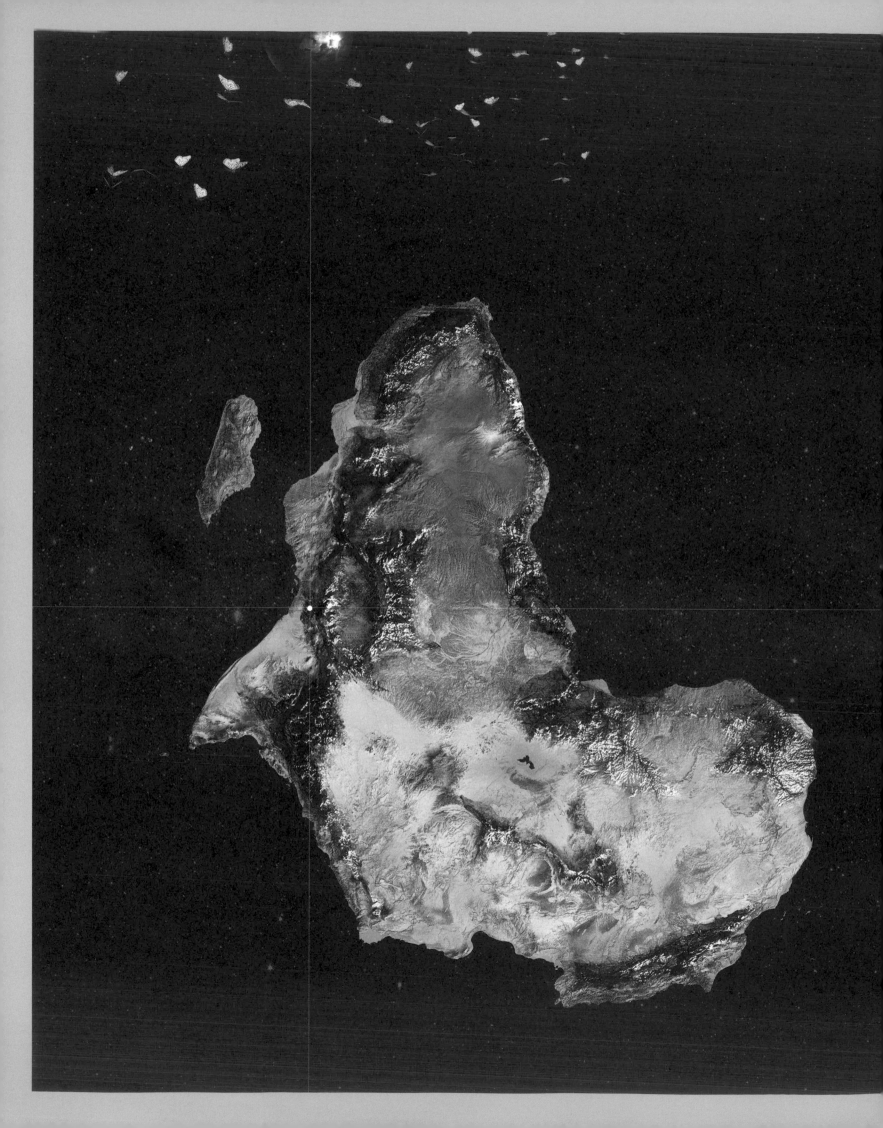

Binadamucene

**Introduction by
Kabage Karanja and Stella Mutegi
of Cave_bureau**

Binadamu (bi-na-da-mu) *noun*: Swahili, meaning human being.

In what might be described as a polite East African opening, we cordially preface this introduction by stating that if you are looking to find a large catalogue of beautiful buildings – a befitting accompaniment to this humbling invitation to participate in the exhibition series *The Architect's Studio* at Louisiana Museum of Modern Art – then we confess you might be in for a disappointment. So, feel free at this early juncture to rest this book back on the coffee table or shelve, whence it came.

However, if you wish to continue, we invite you to consider the practice of architecture as potentially more than the construction of buildings – as beautiful and functional as they may be – and think critically about the agitating origins of architecture itself before we built anything at all, both in thought and in physical form. To do this we must take you back in time, when our early quarter-of-a-million-year-old *homo sapiens* states of cognition crystallised under the open savannah plains with celestial roofs of stars and planets, forest canopies of intimate ecological scale, walled valleys of flow and migration, undulating desert floors of transformation, seas of expansive connection, to archetypal caves of transcendence and origin – this being a small part of the broader context of our collective ancestry that is referred to as the cradle of humankind in East Africa.

Furthermore, if you are keen to reflect on what architecture has to do with questioning our so-called civilisation that is epitomised today by world wars, inequality, racism, ongoing settler occupation, crimes against humanity, species extinction, climate change induced environmental degradation, specifically where the practice of architecture has become unacceptably complicit, or simply passive to the planetary problems we face today, then by all means read on.

We describe ourselves as a bureau of architects and researchers, charting explorations into architecture and urbanism within nature. Akin to a news bureau or government institution responsible for collecting and/or distributing news or information, we collate and coordinate architectural works that address the anthropological and geological context of the African city as a means to confront the com-

plexities of our contemporary rural and urban lives. Operating from Nairobi, Kenya, we are driven to develop systems and structures that aspire to improve the human condition, without negatively impacting the natural environment and social fabric of our communities. To begin this, we navigate a return to the limitless curiosity of our early ancestors, conducting playful and intensive research studies into caves within our capital, Nairobi; around our native Kenya; and different parts of the world. These studies form part of a broader decoding of pre- and postcolonial conditions of the city and its rural hinterland, explored through our imaginations using drawing, storytelling, construction and the curation of performative events of resistance.

The Anthropocene Museum: ushering in a new age Africana
Africana (af-ri-kan-uh) *noun*: Artefacts or artistic or literary works of any of the nations of Africa reflecting geographical, historical or cultural development.

Repetition as having-been-ness is the consideration of the past not as a static event, not as a chronologically fixed date which we can bring to our own age by mere visual or formal invocation, but of searching the possibilities that would have been in the creative work of our ancestors.[1] – Araya Asgedom, architect

Welcome to Africa, the land of our collective ancestral origin, where the human species evolved in a place of natural – and by disjointed extension – architectural beauty of cultural and mythical power. It is where our distant ancestors first lived, and where many of us still remain within the rich biosphere of land, water and air, framed by free radical states of cultural consciousness that connect both scientific and spiritual modes of being on the planet. It is in these interlinked natural states of existence we thrived, as a multitude of communities and civilisations, for it was here the imperial and colonial machinery was at its most effective at attacking our ties to the Earth and its systems of replenishment and healing. To quote the late African-British artist Khadija Saye (1992-2017), "We exist in the marriage of physical and spiritual remembrance. It is in these spaces that we identify with our physical and imagined bodies."[2] The precolonial African consciousness is a spiritual one that connects culture, society and our environment – a "spirituality, which acknowledges that beliefs and practices touch on and inform every facet of human life, and therefore African religion cannot be separated from the everyday or mundane."[3] This during imperial and colonial times was fractured but indeed never broken, instead infused into the many faith systems introduced on the continent over millennia.

As we take a further step back, varyingly hued beings, of minute melanin difference, we migrated from Africa as one shade of colour through what at Cave_bureau we called the corridor of humanity, better known as the Great Rift Valley. From here our *homo sapiens* ancestors crossed what is today known as the Arabian Peninsula approximately sixty to ninety thousand years ago, while our earlier hominin ancestors such as the *homo erectus* are recorded crossing much earlier, almost two million years ago. This geographical wonder of the world was the defining cradle-climate and environment, formed by large subterranean forces that tore the earth's crust, with fault lines pushing up molten rock over thirty-five million years ago. These processes then generated fertile grounds that allowed many creatures to emerge and indeed thrive, stretching from the earliest hominin genus, to us humans constituting only 0.01 percent of the biomass on earth, compared to the vast multitude of animals, birds, plants, insects, bacteria, viruses and so on. Today it remains as one of the most biodiverse environments on the planet.

We ground ourselves to write in this way, as the historian and anthropologist Cheikh Anta Diop (1923-1986), would tell us creative writers on the continent, "because Africa is the cradle of humanity, you are the masters of time. When others enter the world of universal history, you welcome them with open arms because you have already found your rightful place in it."[4] In many ways the Great Rift Valley of East Africa can be referred to as the first laboratory of natural forces at play, an incubator of our human species project. This geological archive afforded us the necessary grounds to move, test, iterate and adapt means to not only exist but thrive on Earth; for better and in-

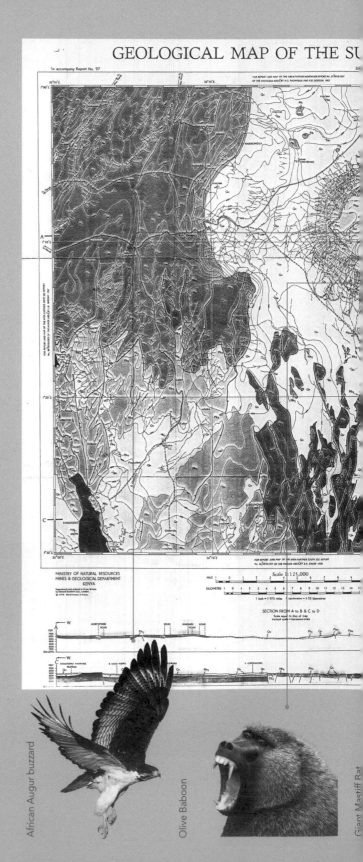

African Augur buzzard

Olive Baboon

deed for worse. At Cave_bureau, we celebrate this territory of origin and grounding from both an anthropological and geological perspective, but critically from an architectural one, which follows the logical path to realign our truncated history of architecture beyond the constraining timelines of human civilisation, to a more-than-human expansive one.

Over the brief time of human existence compared to our four-and-a-half-billion-year-old planet, we have come full circle back to Africa, although in different circumstances and time frames. Over the last five thousand years, the continent of Africa has seen a staggered reverse in human migration back to the homeland, less ventured back by foot, but more so in maritime and recently by air. Historically these were expeditions of exploration and indeed conquest that have a long legacy of human-induced extraction and conflict that span the shores of the easterly Indian Ocean, the Persian Gulf, those of the Mediterranean and the western Atlantic Ocean. Most of this was led by both benevolent and conquering travellers of the fairer kind with migratory legacies harkening back to the ancient civilisations of Mesopotamia, China, India, Persia, Greece, Rome, Arabia, to modern day Europe. Journeys of exploration and trade of spices, wild animals, minerals from the earth, and indeed people through slavery from all corners of the continent, until its so-called abolition in 1834, less than two centuries ago.

Over this time however, perpetually powered by the Industrial Revolution, this reverse in migration was concertedly operationalised on a larger scale of expedition and control at the Berlin conference of 1884, also known as the Scramble for Africa or Partition for Africa. This is where the wretched imperial and colonial project was cast in full motion on a vast geographical and geological scale, not limited to this continent. This was a period of unimaginable exploitation and trauma, more so for humans with skin of the darker kind, but equally those of the fairer kind, who read the neoliberalist injustices at play for what they were, spanning centuries with little if any cessation, redress or reparation. Torture, violence, racial hatred and immorality constitute a dead weight on the so-called civilised, pulling the master class deeper and deeper into the abyss of barba-

Candelabra tree (Euphorbia ingens)

Leopard (Panthera)

rism.[5] The instruments of colonial power, still in operation today, rely on barbaric, brutal violence and intimidation, and the result is the degradation of the Global North itself.[6] Its hesitance to meaningfully confront this legacy in a reparative way only further degrades the human project, with commemorative monuments of architecture only compounding this malaise. As focussed on in our Anthropocene Museum 1.0 project, *Of Steam and Struggle*, we highlight one such record where historian Lotte Huges (born 1952) writes, "There is more than a whiff of colonial arrogance in the behaviour of major global north lenders who invested heavily in the geothermal industry at Ol Karia, in Kenya, the latter since the early 1980s"[7]. Ol Karia is a site where gross environmental impacts of this industry on the local community and this place of natural beauty and biodiversity has been reported.

The Anthropocene

On a technical side, the term 'Anthropocene' was coined in the year 2000 by Nobel Laureate Paul J. Crutzen (1933-2021), it was later built on by other scientists such as Jan Zalasiewicz, Jaia Syvitsky, Mark Williams and Naomi Oreskes, among many others through the Anthropocene Working Group (AWG) of the Subcommission on Quaternary Stratigraphy (SQS) in 2009.[8] Stratigraphy is the branch of geology that studies rock layers, with the SQS being the constituent body that falls under the main International Commission on Stratigraphy and subject to the International Union of Geological Sciences.[9] It is under this hierarchical stratum that the AWG have tasked themselves to formally determine and present the merit of the Anthropocene as a potential new unit of the geological time scale on the International Chronostratigraphic Chart.[10]

The Anthropocene is a proposed epoch of time in which humans have come to dominate a multitude of surface geological processes, with sufficient evidence to suggest it is a real geological phenomenon, and formalised within the Geological Time Scale.[11] The growing consensus that it started around the mid-twentieth century and the post-World War II 'Great Acceleration' of population, industry and resource use,[12] is further grounded in our work, where we read the

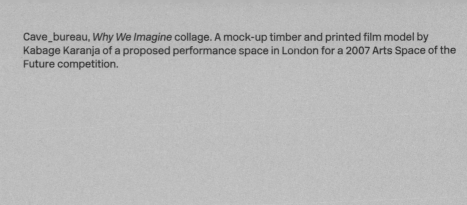

Cave_bureau, *Why We Imagine* collage. A mock-up timber and printed film model by Kabage Karanja of a proposed performance space in London for a 2007 Arts Space of the Future competition.

multitude of decolonial movements across the planet that specifically took place on the land of our collective origin, as a reckoning in return and final reflection during this exact same period. It is where a significant segment of human beings resisted and continue to resist the ongoing anthropogenic pressures faced on the planet. There is an increase in scale of human impacts on the Earth system such as the 120 parts per million rise in CO_2 above pre-industrial levels, while the 'Great Acceleration' interval is also marked by key, near-synchronous stratigraphic markers that identify a putative Anthropocene epoch. All accelerating us closer to a sixth mass extinction event.

As scientifically technical as the whole process might seem, it is not too difficult to consider the broader, ontological and epistemological gravity of such a concept especially from an African vantage point of origin. The entire existence of humankind on planet Earth is framed by an agreed new geological age, defined of course by us humans, and especially by humans from the Global North, conveniently without any meaningful consultation of the majority in the South, who were and still are the least responsible for the devastating coming of this age.[13]

Why we imagine

The neurological reality of our capacity to imagine has been a major causal factor in making *homo sapiens* the dominant species on Earth.[14] At Cave_bureau, we reflect on an abridged history of civilisation where the human brain imagined ways to coexist within the natural world, as investigated in our work, by inhabiting caves through to the Neolithic Revolution right up to the present and recent past where we have imagined ways to colonise the world with little regard for the natural systems that support us. Catapulted by misappropriated Darwinian principles of origin and evolution, we ushered in the exploitation of natural resources that included human beings, taken as slaves, and of colonised peoples that fuelled the Industrial Revolution, who over time also imagined decolonising states of being and existence, feeding a long legacy of resistance that continues right up to today.

As the Cameroonian historian, political theorist, and public

intellectual Achille Mbembe (born 1957) states in his book *Critique of Black Reason* (2013), "race, at once image, body, and enigmatic mirror, is the expression of resistance to multiplicity, and an act of imagination as much as an act of misunderstanding."[15] He addresses the toxic imperial and colonial histories that created and reinforced race around the world, and indeed the age we live in, that favour the few against the many, speaking of the need to read the "giant necropolis of racial capitalism that rests on the traffic of the dead and human bones."[16]

The history of the Anthropocene, where humans have become the dominant force on the Earth, has been described as a perpetual and ongoing state of derangement in the world today, where the Indian author Amitav Ghosh (born 1956) in his 2016 book, *The Great Derangement: Climate Change and the Unthinkable*, says that the climate crisis is also a crisis in culture and thus of the imagination.

Using our imagination again, we look to create a counter force to these realities of our past and present, with a drive in the research and practice of architecture to expand the decolonial legacies of our forefathers and mothers. To survive discursively and physically, but also speak of a new kind of being that is more inclusive and conscious about the nature of repair required to reverse this cognitive malaise that should return us back again to the cave, where we were, and can be in perfect balance with the natural systems of earth again.

More directly, we also look to reconcile the disjointed and often purely human-centred areas of generational exchange and knowledge production within academia and practice. This forms the bedrock of our imaginations, where we work with multiple schools of architecture around the world, to write and teach. Our evolving objective is to better bridge the uneasy gap between these two positions, especially from an African and inclusively decolonial standpoint.

Why we go into caves

Caves as geological structures and spaces are ingrained in our prehistoric consciousness. For over a quarter-of-a-million years of our early hominin and human existence, they have influenced the way we

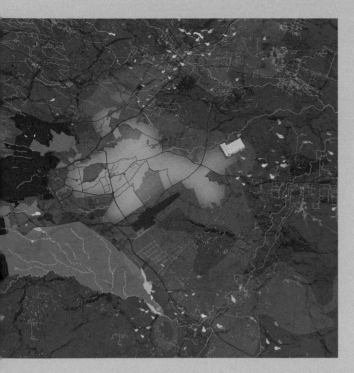

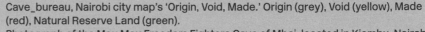

Cave_bureau, Nairobi city map's 'Origin, Void, Made.' Origin (grey), Void (yellow), Made (red), Natural Reserve Land (green).
Photograph of the Mau Mau Freedom Fighters Cave of Mbai, located in Kiambu, Nairobi.

perceive and define the world around us. Humankind's early experience of inside and out, the nave, light wells, shafts, chambers, echoes, among many other architectural experiences and features, can only be directly connected to our ancestor's encounter with caves and associated networks across the ages. Recorded histories of religious revelations within caves, synonymous with the ancient African, Native American, Abrahamic, Hindu, Buddhist, among many other faiths, to philosophical metaphors and narratives about emergence from caves, such as Plato's (427-347 BCE) *Allegory of the Cave*, have formed an intrinsic part of our past, present and future.

As we look today at the postcolonial African city, buildings or modern-day caves made by both men and women have broadened onto a rural and urban network with varying degrees of complexity. At Cave_bureau, we look at the built environment, under three categories: Origin, Void and Made. What we refer to as the Origin is the rural paradigm that most humans inhabited for millennia, but that in recent time, many people leave behind as they migrate towards urban centres. In the city of Nairobi, as in many parts of the world, most of those origin folks end up living in slums and neglected neighbourhoods that function autonomously outside municipal control. These areas of the urban fabric are what we call the Void, the informal heart of the city, usually where the majority of city-dwellers live, often neglected by the nation state, and capitalist driven economies. The last category we designate is the Made, which are parts of the city conveniently appropriated after independence by the "national bourgeoisie, or as it were, an under-developed middle class," as the political philosopher Frantz Fanon (1925-1961) describes. Today, the Made remains the preserve for the more wealthy members of society to live and work. Each of these three territories is complex and interdependent, contradictory, yet rich in their own intricacies and beauties. Understood as a whole, however, they represent and operate in a state of dysfunction, characterised by inequality and poor planning. Our work is drawn to decode these territories as a means to unpack the systems and structures that govern human and non-human life in and outside the decolonised African City.

Equally, caves as habitable spaces and structures are nature's

true and pure manifestation of the museum, by virtue of the fact that on their walls, and within their spaces, moments of cultural and historical importance are enshrined. As one of the earliest cave paintings in Indonesia, the Maros-Pangkep karst in South Sulawesi, Indonesia, depict several human figures hunting pigs in the caves dated at over 43,900 years old. And even older in the Maltravieso cave in Caceres, Spain, paintings made by our closest human relatives, the Neanderthals, sixty-four thousand years ago, which also depict animals against a backdrop of fascinating geometrical frames. Our insistence on studying and experiencing caves that geologically date back millions of years is a celebration of a rich architectural heritage of cave inhabitation by our early and more recent ancestors. Our recent geological histories and theories of architecture have inadequately framed this canon as such, erasing from them the seldom-investigated origin of our first encounter of architecture.

The museum as a cave in these early cultural and material manifestations has changed over varying geological timelines. This simple connection allows us to better reflect on the proposed geological age we live in, the Anthropocene, which brings this anthropological and geological relationship to the fore, requiring more holistic modes of inquiry surrounding the city and nature itself.

Our work is an exploration into this relationship, where we look for sensitive ways to re-think, re-read, re-define architecture on the continent of Africa, and indeed further afield. It is a more-than-human history of architecture we speak of, especially from an Indigenous grounding of what has come to be called animism, which overturns the culturally and environmentally toxic distinctions between the animate and inanimate, living and non-living. It is here we postulate that our earliest human and hominin experiences of caves were architectural in the simplest form of consciousness. Here we encountered a multitude of creatures, materials and atmospheres that we then consciously or subconsciously metamorphosed geologically to produce the artefact of architecture itself – an unrefined geology that needed and still needs constant reference back to the source to create a condition of co-living that is less human-centred but instead more-than-human in nature.

AM
Museum & Monuments Map
Global site context

Maasai Cow Corridor
Nairobi & London 2021

AM 6.0 / Milan Design Week
Freedom Forest
Italy 2022

East Africa

AM 1.0 / Suswa Mountain & Cooper-Hewitt
Of Soccer & Struggle
Suswa & New York 2019

AM 2.0 / Guggenheim Museum & TWA
Shimoni Slave Caves
Shimoni Kwale & New York 2020

AM 4.0 / Dezeen & 15 London & Nairobi
Maasai Cow Corridor
Nairobi & London 2021

AM 6.0 / Festa Parks & Oddut Forest Nairobi
Freedom Forest 2022
Nairobi Kenya

AM 8.0 / Suswa Mountain Kenya
Steam Harvester
Kwale do County Kenya 2023

AM 10.0 / Recraft Institute & Slow Research
Reversing Water Scarcity
Waters of Ol' Donyo Nyokie
Suswa Mountain, Kenya 2023

MIDDLE EAST
Sharjah Triennial

AM 9.0 The Old Sharjah Slaughterhouse Tour

Why the museum?

In our own lifetime, however, we have become aware that the background is no longer just a background. We are part of it, acting as a geological force and contributing to the loss of biodiversity that may, in a few hundred years, become the sixth great extinction. Irrespective of whether the term is ever formalised or not, the Anthropocene signifies the extent and the duration of our species' modification of the earth's geology, chemistry, and biology.[17] – Dipesh Chakrabarty, historian, author and professor

We conceived of The Anthropocene Museum against this background from a geological perspective, as an institution brought into existence by our decimating deposits and extractions on land, ocean and air that have affected the planet. Human beings, predominantly of the fairer kind, have generated a new so-called technosphere, the biosphere's evil twin, which is perpetually altering the Earth system to our own detriment and the rest of life on Earth.[18] We find it myopic, and overly human-centred, to embody this reading of a living museum of the Anthropocene in a single, self-gratifying building, which would be part of an industry that contributes over 40 percent of CO_2 emissions into the atmosphere. We resist this seemingly inevitable by-product of architecture as though there is nothing wrong with the Anthropocene in the first place. In this regard, we challenge the dominant Western conception and operation of the Anthropocene, and architecture from an African Indigenous perspective that relies less on a physical manifestation of the new proposed age but harkens back to our beyond-zero carbon heritages of indigeneity; also looking at generating institutional means and programmes driven to imaginatively reverse it, and drastically thin it out at the same time.[19]

We seek to ground an oral archive in reference to the American historian Saidiya Hartman's (born 1961) work on a critical fabulation, as described in her seismic essay *Venus in Two Acts* (2008), where the sites of our deepest trauma and erasure become the sites of deepest healing.

How does one revisit the scene of subjection without replicating the grammar of violence?[20] – Saidiya Hartman, historian and author

Now to speak of the grammar of geology as Kathryn Yusoff does, which are further enacted using tools of healing that architecture can uniquely exercise on a planetary scale of re-imagination. Kathryn Yusoff is a professor of inhuman geography at Queen Mary University of London and author of the seminal book *A billion black Anthropocenes or Non* (2018), among other publications. We continually reference her work, such as when we constructed a syllabus for Columbia University's Graduate School of Architecture Planning and Preservation (GSAPP), elaborated in this catalogue in The Anthropocene Museum 5.0 section, *Reinscribing New York City*. Her essay in this publication titled *Ancestral Urbanisms of the Anthropocene* presents for us an illuminating means to further theoretically ground our work in the ongoing process to reimagine the museum and city of Nairobi itself, looking at ways to recalibrate the postcolonial African urban fabric for future generations of both human and more-than-human life to thrive.

Also in this catalogue, architect and executive director Joy Mboya's contribution titled *Culture Postponed? Postcolonial Arts and Culture Institution Building in Kenya*, describes how Kenya, after it gained its independence in 1963, 'inherited' key cultural institutions from the colonial state: the National Museums of Natural History and Ethnography, the Kenya Conservatoire of Music and the Kenya National Theatre, among others. Over time, these institutions evolved with relatively minor adjustment, with most remaining constrained within their institutional heritages, struggling up until today to survive without government subsidies, even before the impacts of the COVID-19 pandemic were felt. Compounding this, private museums are permissible, however, the laws of the land dictate that "no person shall operate a museum except in accordance with a license granted by the Minister, which shall be subject to such terms and conditions as the Minister may think fit."[21] Such measures to protect the sites of cultural heritage and reproduction are reasonable and yet are operationalised in a draconian way; these rules are in need of

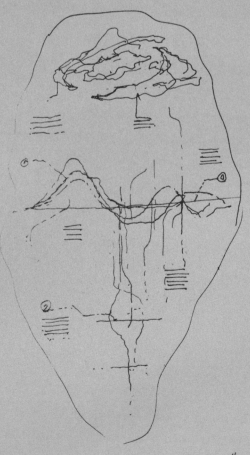

Leakey Fossil
drawings.

cave_bureau

reconstitution to reimagine new ways these institutions can better serve the wider population in the future, while being self-sustaining.

Reverse curation through reverse architecture

No longer perceived as an inheritance or imposition from the West, the museum of the future will have latitude to assume authentically regional forms and functions.[22] – András Szántó, sociologist, author and cultural advisor

András Szántó, sociologist by education, being an author and advisor to museums, foundations and educational institutions, and leading brands worldwide on cultural strategy, interviewed us for his recently published book titled *Imagining the Future Museum* (2022). We spoke about the birth of The Anthropocene Museum, using and indeed misusing the conventions of colonially rooted museology to conceive of and operationalise a new institution across the African continent and beyond. Szántó generously agreed to publish the interview in this catalogue.

The Anthropocene Museum is visible on the map, as depicted earlier, of all museum institutions and monuments across the entire planet. We regard these as critical geological markers that represent the material manifestation of our extractive cultural value systems, including artefacts, arts works, installations, events of cultural significance and so on, predominantly encased or entombed in built form. These structures are representative of most social, cultural, political and indeed economic states of meaning and significance across the globe, circled and without clearly drawn borderlines, defining in their own right the continental masses of land, especially those of the Global North, less of the Global South. The sparse amorphous areas of the south remain in most part as sites of neoliberalist exploitation and extraction, where inherited colonial museums or their embedded cousins remain aloof to these realities and seemingly intent on remaining in a state of rigor mortis, unable to change and suit present day audiences, or indeed hindrances to new forms of cultural institution building and reproduction of reimagined heritage.

In the north, museums are warehouses of stolen loot, as

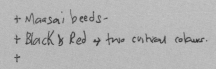

+ Maasai beeds-
+ Black & Red → two cultural colours.
+

PROCESS.
+ descriptive.
locations of
Museum site.

+

- Tv WRAP.

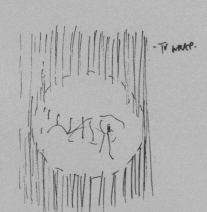

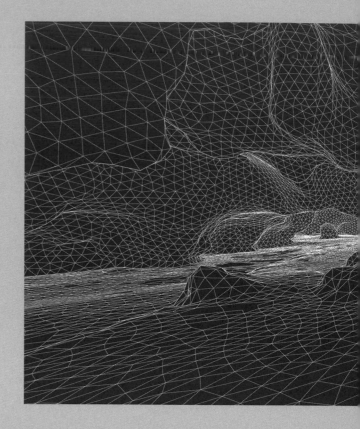

American anthropologist Anna Tsing (born 1952) calls them – for even those without a direct link to the imperial and colonial times are conjoined in the dance of material extraction and environmental degradation. The Anthropocene Museum in this regard presents the reality of our times, a moral reckoning of sorts that operates and registers at this scale of repair to address the extent of the challenge we face as a species. Critically, without using past grammars, we operationalise our imaginations through a museum-remaking programme that is both confrontational and reparative, taking place of course over a multitude of museums and cultural institutions, and indeed the natural background that we are part of. Simultaneously, we critique what a 'museum' is understood to be, represent, contain, and operate as.

Together, these critiques point to the stark inadequacies of recent geological histories and framings of architecture. For us using them in this context is an act of reclamation. It is a way of reflecting on and reframing an epoch with an operational logic that has been to ravage the Earth in the interest of growing economies, manifesting so-called leaps of civilisation like the Industrial Revolution and continuing today through an encompassing neoliberalist expansion project across the globe. These pressures have fundamentally brought about the climate emergency we now face that poses an existential threat to life on Earth. The museum in this context is no longer registered as an innocuous institution that innocently serves to feed the public's appetite to experience cultural reproduction, but instead a potent institution that must reflect on the vast territory of our presently deficient human culture that needs a thorough reckoning and reimagining, curated in reverse through acts of collective repair and reverse architecture. We use modern day point cloud three-dimensional laser scanning technology, to survey caves and natural phenomena in different parts of the world where we work with communities that live around them, transposing their geometries in different states and locations, both in the material and immaterial sense, and also reigniting our past cognitive structures of cohabitation with other species that were always parametrically complex, and adequate enough to navigate back towards.

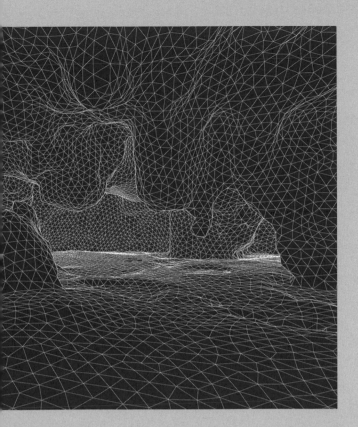

Cave_bureau, point cloud laser scanning of Shimoni Slave Caves.

The Anthropocene Museum here takes on the ongoing task of what we refer to as reverse curation, addressing the current narrative about the return/restitution of stolen artefacts from Africa. We resist the condescending actions and indeed inaction of museums of half-truths, half-heartedly imagining the return of stolen artefacts, or museums of full truths, with half-actions that appear to educate well but narrate our histories in pacifying ways, without a sense of urgency to speed up the repair. In this catalogue of our museum programmes we demonstrate the partnerships and morevoer the collective sense of responsibility that can bring museum institutions together through meaningful dialogue that not only manifests in exhibitions but in impactful exercises of collaborative healing.

Ngaire Blankenberg, the now former director of the Smithsonian's National Museum of African Art (NMAFA) has been transforming the museum, in her own words, with a vision for a more global and distributed museum, that can provide experiences for people all over the world. We had the honour to be invited as advisors for the exciting new phase of the museum's future in this proposed age of the Anthropocene. In this catalogue, Ngaire Blankenberg is formulating a fluid museum, which is beyond bridge building across fractured lands and human histories. She boldly reimagines how the cave-natured anatomy of NMAFA can become a living reconnection with the communities on the continent of Africa, its diaspora and indeed the global public, both ambitious and timely in this age of perpetual crisis. She reignites the subject of diversity in museum institutions, grounding reverse curation through meaningful engagement with communities that continue to receive returned stolen artefacts, and ultimately challenging perceived distinctions between the scientific and spiritual realms of cultural production of material and immaterial artefacts that were always interlinked in our collective African states of consciousness and capable of growing on a global scale of operation and impact.

If it is no longer sufficient to expose the scandal, then how might it be possible to generate a different set of descriptions from this archive? To imagine what could have been? To envision a free state from this order of statements? [...] I longed to write a new story, one unfettered by the constraints of the legal documents and exceeding the restatement and transpositions, which comprised my strategy for disordering and transgressing the protocols of the archive and authority of its statements and which enabled me to augment and intensify its fictions.[23] – Saidiya Hartman, historian and author

We are not alone!

In other words, the ongoing journey of our research and praxis has never been taken individually. We are in the warm company of profound thinkers and makers who drive us forward, some of whom have passed on to the celestial plains of our ancestors, and some who still dwell here. We have called upon some of them as invited guest-authors and some recognised in quotes and footnotes, who in their own right have garnered critical acclaim around the world. These are people we hold dear as mentors and guides, some of whom not only speak on our research and practice that has been in gestation for almost ten years, but in a few cases take this opportunity within the context of our research to open up new lines of inquiry in their own work.

We have already mentioned professor Kathryn Yusoff, sociologist András Szántós, directors Joy Mboya and Ngaire Blankenberg, who have generously contributed to this catalogue and last but not least we will mention in gratitude Mark Williams, Jan Zalasiewicz and Lesley Lokko. Mark Williams and Jan Zalasiewicz, both British professors of palaeobiology at Leicester University, are as previously stated among a group of scientists who put forth the first proposal to adopt the Anthropocene epoch as a formal geological interval. Triggered by a round table forum in Johannesburg organised by Lesley Lokko, and in the spirit of cross-disciplinary practice, we sent an email in 2017 to Jan Zalasiewicz about our work and interest in reaching out. To our surprise, he replied a few days later and introduced us to his colleagues Mark Williams and Sarah Gabbott, who after a few months travelled to Kenya to jointly investigate one of the largest landfill sites in Africa, the Dandora Dump site, which we had recommended. We continued to keep in touch, so it was natural for us to invite them to contribute to this publication in the spirit of their ongoing research surrounding the Anthropocene. The essay by Mark Williams, Jan Zalasiewicz and PhD student Molly Desorgher on the hidden underground rivers of London reveals more about their work.

We cannot overstate the significance of professor Lesley Lokko OBE, an architect, academic and bestselling novelist, formerly dean of architecture at the City College of New York and founder and director of the African Futures Institute, AFI Accra in Ghana. She is also the Curator of the 18th Venice Biennale of Architecture (2023), titled *The Future Laboratory*.

The laboratory inevitably conveys mysterious significance, it appears as a cave of sorts, where a (necessarily) solitary genius is pursuing some fantastic goal. To the society at large, the laboratory seems much like the mediaeval den of an alchemist.[24] – Souleymane Bachir Diagne, philosopher

Lesley Lokko is that kind of genius, and modern-day African Matri(arch) whose work in academia and practice deeply informs and resonates with us and many, within and outside the profession. As invited participants to the Venice Biennale this year (2023), we thought it critical to muster up the courage to ask her for an interview. With the help of Louisiana Museum of Modern Art, she gracefully obliged and invited us to her home in Accra. From the onset we gladly observed all African protocols and rightly reiterate how her work deeply influences ours and in particular the free radical nature of our research that it has become synonymous with, akin to a scorpion as she describes in the interview. We see the formulation of Lokko's *Future Laboratory* as a grounded extension of the enigmatic work of the Senegalese historian Cheikh Anta Diop, among other thinkers and makers, but particularly when it concerns 'the African origin of civilisation', and where Diop states that he intends to harness the scientific potential and creativity of the Black world and place it at the disposal of all Black states without distinction.[25] We read the flourishing meadow, or *uwanja* in Swahili, of networks and

real relational linkages Lokko creates, which are neither constrained by race nor ignorant of its presence in our imaginations.

It should be said that in 2017 Lokko indirectly introduced us to the Anthropocene for the first time, during a round table forum that she organised in Johannesburg, South Africa. One of the invited guests, political theorist Achille Mbembe (born 1957), outlined how impossible it would be to talk about the future of Africa and its complicated history, without investigating this proposed unofficial unit of geological time when humans, and especially *some* humans for that matter, became actors on a vast global scale of influence and impact. This forum took place exactly nine years after the AWG in 2008 put forth the first proposal to adopt the Anthropocene epoch as a formal geological interval. It was an important decision for Cave_bureau to focus on this research topic that is still a contested subject of ongoing debate. From the logic of its naming as the age of humankind – there are counter-proposals to instead call it the Chthulucene, Capitalo-cene or Plantationcene – to debates about when exactly it is believed to have begun, to questions about who was responsible for bringing this age into being in the first place, among other seismic critiques. Six years on, it has proven to be a productive area of ongoing research and investigation, but importantly a site to fertilise our imaginations.

Reticulation of the Anthropocene through the Binadamu Addendum

Reticulate (re-tic-u-late) *verb*: Divide or mark (something) in such a way as to resemble a net or network.

At the heart of our research and practice, we argue two things: firstly, that the Anthropocene, originally from the Greek word *ánthrōpos*, meaning "human being" and *cene* meaning "new or recent," fused to describe the age of the human being, should indeed be used verbatim as proposed by the AWG of the International Union of Geological Sciences. This, however, should not be done without an equalising and eventually superseding open addendum that we call the Binadamu Addendum, which adopts the Swahili word for human being, in a language whose origins harken from East Africa and

predominantly comprised of Bantu, which is of African lineage, fused with the Arabic trading language. It spread to over fourteen countries, with seven in Africa today using it as a national language.

The Binadamu Addendum will be a living archive of oral and written histories and futures, containing a compendium of works such as Anna Tsing's *Feral Atlas* (2021), *Staying with the Trouble: Making Kin in the Chthulucene* (2016) by American professor emerita Donna Haraway (born 1944) and *The Anthropocene Museum*, among many others. It would constitute a composition of active critiques, where old and new untold stories, which Kathryn Yusoff would argue run in the billions, "apprehend the past in the present colonial mining empires of white settler nations." As she says, stories that frame white geology as a historical regime of material power, not a genetic imaginary, over the past twenty-three years since its millennial conception, needs to come to terms with how this age came into being and to imagine ways to initiate the monumental task of planetary repair of our age.[26]

It signals a reticulated moving mark on the soil of the countering network of stories and mass actions to reverse, if not at least reconfigure the direction of the human project on a geological scale of ongoing destructive heritage – networks and shifts in social consciousness that have manifested in movements such as Black Lives Matter, #MeToo, Stop Asian Hate, Extinction Rebellion, the Sunrise Movement, Rhodes Must Fall, SOS Columbia. These are movements that have their roots in past struggles of resistance such as the civil rights movements in America, the women's suffrage movement in the UK, the Mau Mau Uprising in Kenya, the Anti-Apartheid Movement in South Africa, the Algerian nationalists' movement, the Tiananmen Square protests in China, among many others.

Secondly, we argue for a parallel independent working group that confluences practitioners of programmes and practices for planetary repair to confront all facets of our human project – a project that remains in a perpetual state of derangement as Amitav Ghosh would express it, from the literary, political, economic, in psychology, within the arts and architecture, among many the sciences, which have failed to apprehend this age of negative human impacts on the Earth system. We aim to avoid speaking of repair abstractly and delinked from imperial and colonial histories of subjugation and slavery as though they were disconnected from each other; instead speak in tandem with reparative and restorative actions that can begin with compensation.

The Anthropocene Museum aims to institutionally establish a cultural bedrock of reproduction when reading this new age, in a way that comfortably and inclusively speaks of the historic grammars of violence on a geological scale, where we exist in a perpetual state of climate injustice, but that it can only be repaired collectively as an intentioned Binadamu species. We use our imaginations to set in motion a response to an emergency, to not only exist but also thrive together and generate projects of repair on a global scale, where the possibilities of architectural thought unbowed and no longer limited.

The tools that architects have are infinite. Hilary Mantel, who's one of my favourite writers, died yesterday. She was asked by the Financial Times *earlier this month whether she believed in an afterlife. Mantel said she did, but that she couldn't imagine how it could work: 'However, the universe isn't limited by what I can imagine'.*[27] – Lesley Lokko, professor

Passed on ...
Khadija Saye
Frantz Fanon
Edward Said
Michel Foucault
Wangari Mathai
Dedan Kimathi
Tom Mboya
Aimé Césaire
Jean-Paul Sartre
W.E.B. Du Bois
Charles Darwin
Michel Foucault
Markus Fairs
Cheikh Anta Diop

In this space we breathe ...
Demas Nwoko
Ngũgĩ wa Thiong'o
Lesley Lokko
Achille Mbembe
Fred Moten
Saidiya Hartman
Joy Mboya
Kathryn Yusoff
Carolyn Strauss
Ngaire Blankenberg
Mark Williams
Jan Zalasiewicz
Sarah Gabbott
Souleymane Bachir Diagne
Muthoni Wa Kirima
Araya Asgedom
Joseph Conteh

Notes

1 Araya Asgedom, "The Unsounded Space," *White Papers Black Marks: Architecture, Race Culture*, ed. Lesley Lokko (University of Minnesota Press, 2020), 270.

2 David A. Bailey & Jessica Taylor, *Diaspora Pavilion May 13 – November 26, 2017, Palazo Pisani S. Marina Venice*, 42.

3 As described by Professor of Indigenous African religions at Harvard, Jacob Olupona, https://news.harvard.edu/gazette/story/2015/10/thespirituality- of-africa/

4 Souleymane Bachir Diagne, *In the Den of the Alchemist* (Xibaaru, 2018), 20.

5 Aimé Césaire, *Discourse on Colonialism* (1950).

6 Ibid.

7 Read more at https:// www.theelephant.info.

8 Edward Burtynsky, *Anthropocene* (Steidl, 2018), 36.

9 Harriet Harriss and Naomi House, *Working at the Intersection: Architecture After the Anthropocene*, Design Studio Vol. 4. (RIBA Publishing, 2022).

10 Ibid.

11 Ibid.

12 Will Steffen et al., "The Trajectory of the Anthropocene: The Great Acceleration," *The Anthropocene Review* (2015).

13 Harriss and House, *Working at the Intersection*.

14 Joseph Carroll, Mathias Clasen, Emelie Jonsson, *Evolutionary Perspectives on Imaginative Culture* (Springer, 2020).

15 Achille Mbembe, *Critique of Black Reason*, 2013 (Duke University Press, 2017), 110.

16 Ibid., 137.

17 Dipesh Chakrabarty, *The Climate of History in a Planetary Age* (The Univeristy of Chicago Press, 2021).

18 Kabage Karanja & Stella Mutegi, "In practice: Cave Bureau on a museum for the Anthropocene," *The Architectural Review* (April 2021), 79.

19 American professor emerita Donna Haraway writes about our epoch from a multispecies feminist standpoint questioning the term 'Anthropocene' in her 2016 book, *Staying with the Trouble, Making Kin in the Chthulucene*.

20 Saidiya Hartman, *Venus in Two Acts* (Duke University Press, 2008).

21 National Council for Law Reporting, National Museums and Heritage Act, Chapter 216.

22 András Szántó, *Imagining the Future Museum: 21 Dialogues with Architects* (Hatje Cantz, 2022).

23 Hartman: *Venus in Two Acts.*

24 Diagne, *In the Den,* 11.

25 Cheikh Anta Diop, *The African Origin of Civilization – Myths or Reality* (Lawrence Hill & Co. Publishers, 1974).

26 Kathryn Yusoff, *A Billion Black Anthropocenes or None* (University of Minnesota Press, 2019).

27 Lesley Lokko interviewed on p. 194 in this catalogue.

# of Steam and Struggle

The Anthropocene Museum 1.0

We carried out our first expedition along the Great Rift Valley in Kenya, stretching from the Mount Suswa Caves 150 kilometres west of Nairobi city and connecting underground to the Mbai Caves in Kiambu county, 20 kilometres north. Here we made a film that confronts the adverse effects of the geothermal energy extraction practices taking place along the Great Rift Valley by recording critiques from the local community regarding the negative impacts that extraction has had on their lives and on natural ecosystems. The film highlights how the natural and cultural heritage of this territory was, and remains, under threat from the government's voracious appetite to exploit geothermal energy in Suswa, as the country hurtles towards its commitment to power the entire country using green energy.

The caves are home to a great number of wild animal species, such as the 'Baboon Parliament.' This section of the caves is distinguished by a large cave roof collapse, dome-shaped with a ten-meter diameter oculus, which we refer to as the origin of Rome's Pantheon, preceding it by 1.7 million years. We produced drawings and models to depict these similitudes as a way to ground the broader significance of a site seldom reflected on within the mainstream discourse of architecture. The powerful construction process of the lava that burnt through rock following the eruption of Mount Suswa, such as multiple roof collapses across the mountain, allowed light and life to come into the cave as the Pantheon did later. The Pantheon's proportions align with that of the Baboon Parliament on multiple levels. We used the imagined hovering hemisphere in drawing and model to read the rotunda in both settings, and return the reading of architecture to its root, within the Great Rift Valley, where our early ancestors roamed and imagined.

Anthropocene Museum 1.0: *Of Steam and Struggle*, Mount Suswa, Great Rift Valley, Nairobi, Kenya, 2019–2020. Community engagement, short film, cave installation, bronze models, leather drawings, concurrent book publications (*Slow Spatial Reader, Chronicles of Radical Affection* and *An Allegory Of Urbanism in Africa)* and exhibition, Cooper Hewitt Smithsonian Design Museum, New York and Cube Museum Kerkrade, Netherlands.

The short film *The Anthropocene Museum 'Olmanyara'* (meaning "Nature" in Maasai) brings together artist Jackie Karuti (born 1987), local Maasai conservationist Ishmael Nkukuu, the young Maasai herdboy Sirima Kapiani (born 2008) and anticolonial Mau Mau veteran Beatrice Wanjiku (born 1946) to discuss these challenges and think of ways to work with nature to resist environmental and social pressures. We sat with the three invited guests in the temporary bamboo structure made using hybrid measurements based on traditional African building techniques; it also adapts the Fibonacci sequence (in which each number is the sum of the two preceding ones), creating an alternative interpretation of Plato's *Allegory of the Cave*.

Cave_bureau, *Of Steam and Struggle* drawing. The history of Marcus Agrippa's Pantheon in Rome is akin to the history of Mount Suswa's Baboon Parliament, albeit with vastly different timelines, the latter naturally preceding it. Akin to the formations of the lava tube cave in Suswa, the Pantheon went through a tumultuous period of gestation – the mystery of its design is like a natural phenomenon. More intriguingly, there is no architect or architects known to be responsible for its final design in 120 AD under the reign of Emperor Hadrian; it is speculated Apollodorus of Damascus could have been responsible, having completed works of a similar nature, such as Trajan's Forum.
Cave_bureau, Baboon Parliament and Rome's Pantheon drawing.

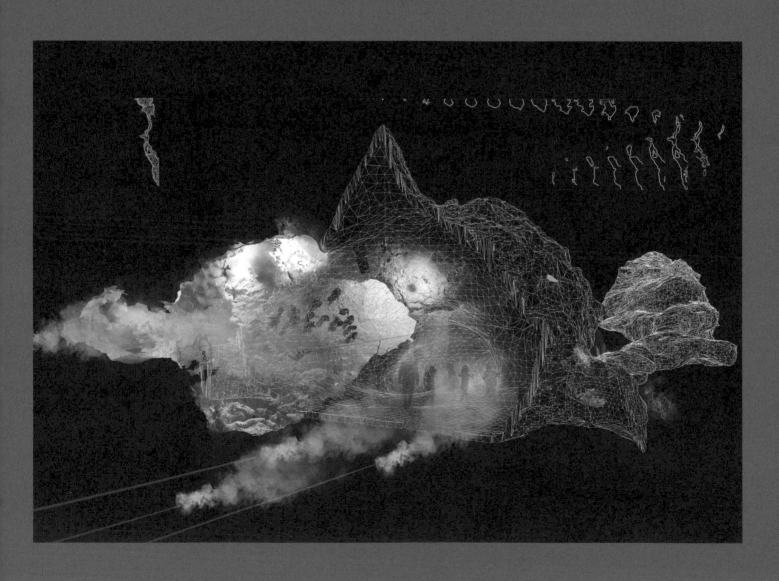

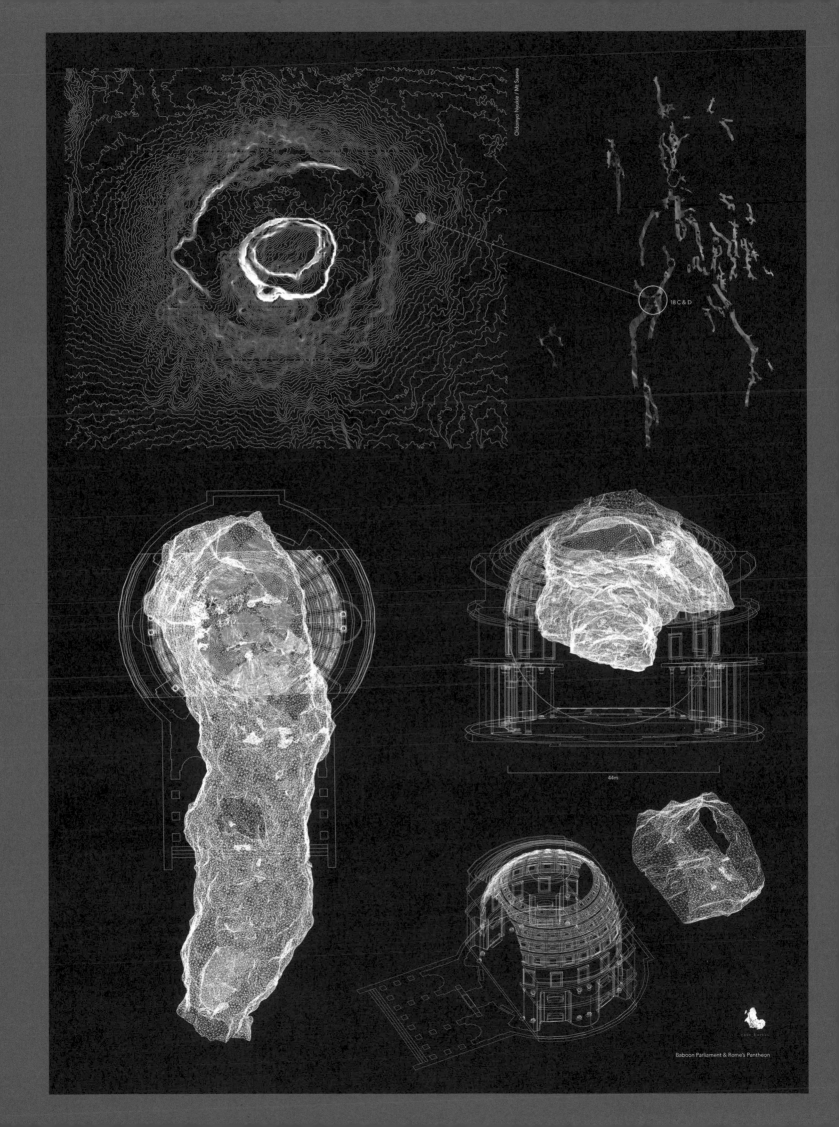

Oldoinyo Nyokie / Mt. Suswa

18 C & D

44m

Baboon Parliament & Rome's Pantheon

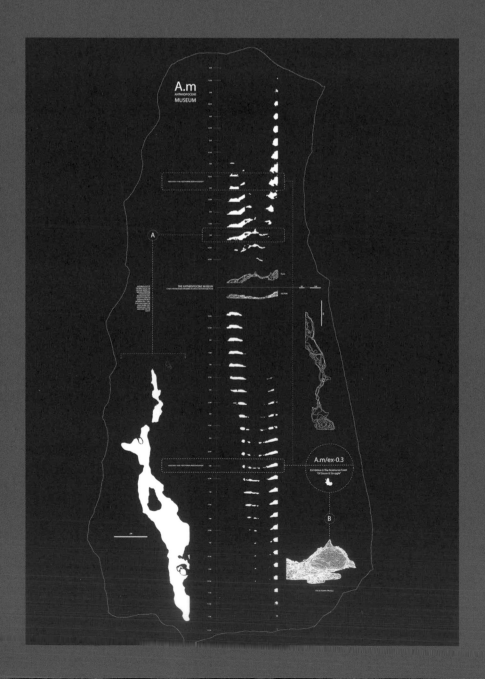

A.m
ANTHROPOCENE
MUSEUM

A.m/ex-0.3

Exhibition 3: the Reclaimed Forest
"Of Steam & Struggle"

A

B

Mau Mau fires

The Nave Slice

Cave_bureau, bronze. The decolonial Mau Mau Freedom Fighters Cave network of Mbai. This architecture of resistance and heritage is where Cave_bureau dared to imagine a new African state for the future. Cave_bureau scanned this lava tube cave in three dimensions, drew it in plan and section, then cast it in bronze at a scale of 1:50, for posterity.

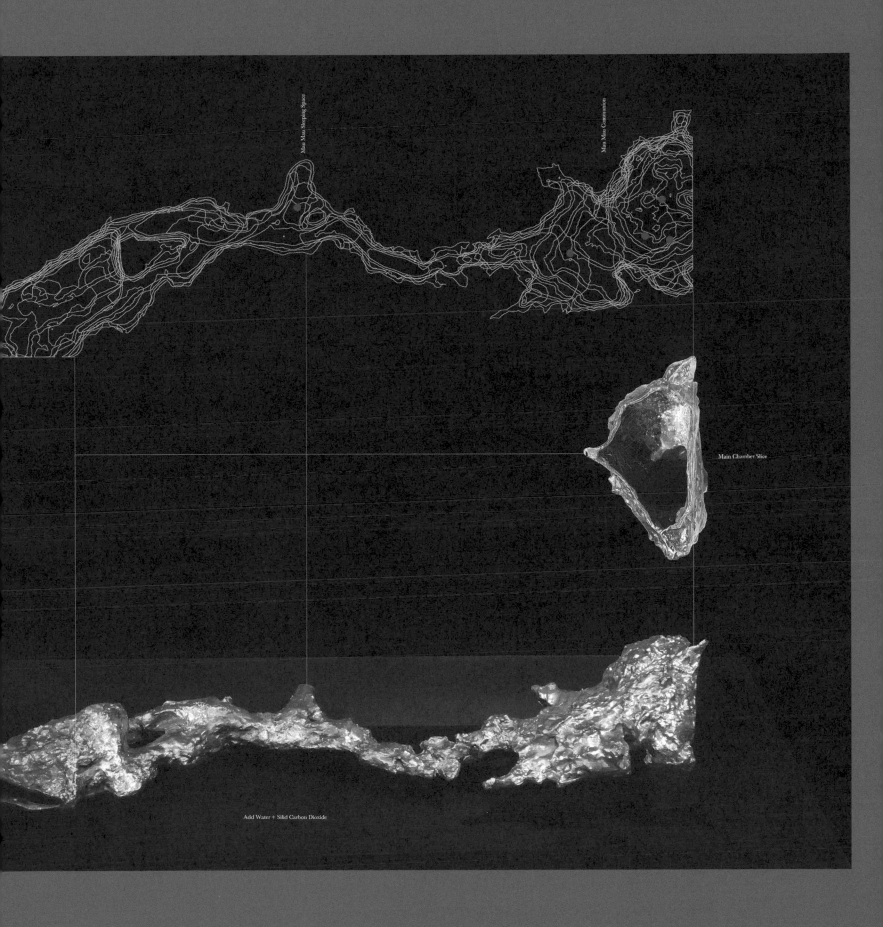

Mau Mau Sleeping Space

Mau Mau Communion

Main Chamber Slice

Add Water + Silid Carbon Dioxide

Things are Going to Go Full Circle

Interview with
Kabage Karanja and Stella Mutegi
by András Szántó

On a hot summer afternoon in 2022, I found myself at Columbia University's Graduate School of Architecture, in a crit session run by Kabage Karanja and Stella Mutegi, founding partners of the Nairobi-based Cave_bureau. The students had just concluded a semester devoted to exploring how the subterranean landscape of natural caves and abandoned human-made infrastructure might offer innovative solutions for urban and environmental resilience in New York City. The projects, including one that envisioned a museum in a derelict subway tunnel, were breathtakingly original. For Karanja and Mutegi, Africa is the perfect launching pad for these ideas. The museum on the continent is inextricably linked to histories of colonial erasure and extraction. Yet Africa is poised to become a laboratory for museum-making. The cave – both as physical space and as metaphor – is a provocation to test the limits of contemporary architecture. It invites new thinking about how the museum can adapt to a more community-focussed ecologically sensitive, low-carbon future.

ANDRÁS SZÁNTÓ *While you have done a lot of thinking about museology, you have not designed a brick-and-mortar museum, at least not yet. How did your partnership come about?*

STELLA MUTEGI We were fired on the same day. We worked together in a big architectural firm. They were laying people off, and we happened to be among those being let go. We went our separate ways, but a few months later we got in touch, and Cave_bureau was born.

– Your official titles are Matri(arch) and Explorer, respectively – not your typical designations in an architecture studio. Can you elaborate?

SM Many young people come to work at Cave with a lot of unlearning to do. Apart from guiding them in their professional careers as architects and researchers, I am also the mother hen in the office. I ask tough questions. I'll expect an answer, and I will not move on until I get one.

KABAGE KARANJA: I am an explorer because I have always taken an interest in going out into the wild. One of my first, most visceral experiences was sleeping in a cave. That framed my philosophy of looking into caves. I do a lot of hunting and thinking about opportunities for us. I bring them to the office and put them on the table with our matriarch, Stella, and we decide what's worth pursuing.

– Your core interest is the anthropological and geological context of the postcolonial African city. What are your observations on the museum, especially the art museum, in the African context?

SM The museum in Africa is problematic. It is an installation of what the colonialists thought the museum should be. Culturally, Africans didn't have museums per se. We had artefacts, rituals and objects, which were not intended for display. We didn't necessarily exhibit things for pleasure or for study. From a colonial point of view, these were alien things of interest to share with others, and this meant displaying them and writing about them. A museum is almost alien to Africa.

KK The contents and practice of museology have been even more problematic from the colonial perspective. They are extractive. The museum is not an innocuous, harmless institution where beautiful objects are simply displayed. Museums have used modes of erasure along the way. It was about de-civilisation and conquest, as aptly described by Kathryn Yusoff in her 2018 book *A Billion Black Anthropocenes or None*. Our equivalent of the museum was more in tune with life and the appreciation of real-time existence, where children were taught what it meant to live in an actual environment and in a community setting. At Cave, we focus on that real-life enactment of practice within Indigenous spaces.

– An emphasis on social gathering is a current preoccupation for museums. So this may be a case where Indigenous ideas can be re-integrated. What do you think?

KK We feel things are going to go full circle. Following the pandemic and given the pressures of environmental destruction, it makes perfect sense for institutions to look at Indigenous practices as new knowledge-making centres to rethink this so-called civilisation. We need to reassess our modes of existence.

– Tell me about the cave as a metaphor, as a set of ideas.

SM You can go back to the cave and start again. The cave was shelter for early man and a space of life expression across stone walls. The cave for us, in the colonial context, was a place where we went back to reclaim our lands, our freedom. It is the place we go back to so we may forge our way into the future – a place of refuge, of refreshment, of origin.

– In this century, the museum seems poised to proliferate on the African continent. How might that fractalise our view of the museum?

KK The architect, author and curator Lesley Lokko has said that Africa is the laboratory of the future. It has the youngest population in the world. There are exciting movements and modes of interaction that will embody new thoughts about what a museum is, should be, can be.

SM Many institutions right now have to grapple with whether they have the moral authority to display the objects in their vast collections. They are questioning how they got them and whether they should return some of them. There is going to be a big shift.

– About The Anthropocene Museum, you have written that it is "an institution of creative action, not constrained by four walls, but generative enough to openly challenge the prevailing status quo – literally from the ground up." [1] *What are the implications?*

SM We call it a roaming museum. We tackle a different issue in every place we have been, such as colonialism or climate change. These are uncomfortable subjects, and for a long time they have been buried. To put it simply: The Anthropocene Museum is an awareness museum that brings to the fore issues that are not comfortable, that require deep discussion and new frameworks to be put in place to resolve.

– Kabage, what does it mean for you?

KK The geological grounding and basis of our thinking are what frames the hardware of the museum. In our Anthropocene Museum 1.0, we were in Mount Suswa, an active volcano in Kenya along the Great Rift Valley. We examined the practice of extracting geothermal power from the ground. The government of Kenya and international organisation such as the World

Bank and United Nations have been complicit in sidelining the local Indigenous people from the benefits of this project. We bring to light these problems. We made installations to talk to the communities within the caves about issues surrounding geothermal energy. It is important for museums to be a lens on culture and society, to question complicated issues that impact the natural environment and the people that live there.

– I like the image of the museum as lens. In a 2008 article, you talk about "liberating and cerebral spaces of refuge that our freedom-fighting forebears inhabited, in particular, caves."[2] This is an African heritage. What can institutions worldwide take away from this line of thinking?

KK People are at the heart of what we do. And people are usually marginalised within the prevailing discourse, including discussions about art and culture. We find it valuable to have discussions with communities that are often left by the wayside in mainstream cultural debates. That would be the takeaway: that at the heart of it, it's not about following the latest trends within any curatorial programme. As Amitav Ghosh [Indian author] has said, the climate crisis is also a crisis of culture, and thus of the imagination. Museums have been, and often still are, problematic players in the Anthropocene, compounding the state of crisis in the world today. Here we simply return instinctively back to caves as our decolonial freedom-fighter ancestors did, to continue reimagining the African state of the future.

– How do you situate the efforts of architects to embed the museum in an African context?

SM They are a bit problematic. These architects are re-creating something that is already problematic. Putting up a building is not the way forward. We need to find creative ways of curating, especially coming from the African context, where much of our history was oral, passed down from generation to generation. A good basis to start would be understanding that a museum in Africa cannot be a fancy building that is going to win you awards.

– Kabage, do you agree that you can't really have conventional museum buildings in Africa – or only with different intentions and modalities?

KK We can, and we will. But for now, we still seem to be using the same software to think about the institution, and it is conjoined to the same hardware, the building. Yes, museums are rethinking how they can be constructed closer to the community – and that is great – but the same economics are at play, and private patrons are financing the museum if the government is not interested, which is the reality in most of Africa. And the private sector is not immune to compromise.

– Physical structures are needed in the context of restitution of heritage artefacts. The Benin Bronzes are headed back to Benin City after spending more than a century dispersed across various European and American museums, partly because new museum infrastructure is being built for them. How do you see this process playing out?

SM It is good to acknowledge that these things are being returned. But they are being returned to a different context – to people who might find them alien, because there has been so much erasure of culture.

Do you put them in a museum? Do you give them back to the community they were taken from? Do those people still value these objects? That is a huge dilemma facing these institutions.

KK It should be said that the artefact-restitution process is still fraught with delay tactics, bad faith, and more than not, condescending bravado. The communities that were directly affected are rarely if ever brought to the table to plan this return, which we term as a disjointed process of reverse curation. Again, we see here the colonial machinery at work, sidelining the primary curators of these artefacts who have the right to decide what they do or don't do with these stolen goods inside or indeed outside the confining walls of the museum building.

– Let's talk about administrative structures. These are likewise legacy elements. How would you redefine the roles of a curator or director? What new roles might have to be invented?

KK I will give you an example. At Mount Suswa, we deal with a conservationist called Ishmael. His knowledge about the geography of the site goes beyond anything we have experienced, as do his sensitivity and closeness to the community. Museums are in no way even in touch with such an individual. You almost wonder: Should the institution remain as it is, and then have such agents who can apply pressure on the institution? Or should the institution be broken up and dispersed into the community, a sort of devolution of its operation, so it can then begin to express what it is about in the context of what is important to them?

– Architecturally, materially, spatially – what would such an institution look like?

KK We gravitated to caves because they are spaces already being used by the community. The people aren't mobilised enough to curate exhibitions in the caves, but there are many caves where this could happen. These spaces of geological relevance would not require us to build much. It would just be about how we curate the space. We recently got an invitation to curate in caves in the United Arab Emirates. This structure is already there. The hardware is there.
　Nature has provided these galleries.

KK Absolutely. And we have been too lazy going a hundred miles an hour, creating these huge buildings with large carbon footprints. For too long we have ignored the original spaces that are there in abundance, tied into communities. That is for us the perfect balance. From our experience, the communities that surround the caves have the historical knowledge that would allow for a close engagement with relevant topics and curatorial exercises with them.

– Given concerns about ecology, is there any justification for new buildings? There are so many existing sites and buildings available.

SM No, I don't think so.

– That's a pretty big statement coming from an architect.

SM We have struggled with some students who don't understand that. One thing Kabage says all the time is, when a client brings a project, you should question whether it even needs to be a building. That is a realm architects need to start thinking about. Architecture is one of the biggest contributors to climate change. We have to start being a bit more responsible, and not just in regard to climate. This is a question I want to ask an architect who wants to create a masterpiece: Have you thought outside of your ego?

– So with all this in mind, not just in the African context, how would you define a museum?

KK It is not what it used to be. Both its software and its hardware need to fundamentally change. The museum was an institution that embodied a lot of trauma. It was complicit in the colonial and imperial project. It needs to become extremely diverse, and I think that is happening. Fundamentally, the institution is going through a crisis. This is not a short, sharp exercise. Architecture is, in fact, at the root of questioning the museum. We need to develop the ability to embed the institution in society. In Kenya, we have dozens of tribes, each of whom have experienced colonisation in multiple ways. How does the museum grapple with that? It's not a simple affair, but it is opening up an opportunity.

SM My definition of the museum is a place that is inclusive and not specific to a particular place. If I am somewhere in a village in Kenya, I can access the same information that someone deep in Argentina is accessing in terms of a curated museum. It is decentralised.

– I would like to come back to this idea of a space where the community is actualised. Can today's museums do that?

KK With the community in mind. And it needs to be where the community is physically located. Museums are institutions of power and economy. As soon as they are centralised, they become about what you have extracted from the communities and brought back to the so-called museum, with its grand architecture. Once you dismantle that centralisation, you open up the museum to all the nuanced context of where the museum resides. We are trying to do that at Mount Suswa, in what you nicely referred to as actualized community space. We unashamedly introduce this new institution as the most critical evolutionary iteration of the museum of the future, in this, our putrid age of crisis, the so-called Anthropocene.

– How should the process of designing museums be different?

SM We have thought about creating what we would call *BRIT*, which stands for "Benevolent Reparations Institute." It would address all those complex issues around whom you are repatriating to, who gets the money, what it is used for. We envision going into the communities, presenting the problem and letting the community come up with how they want the issues addressed. A panel of stakeholders, community leaders, museum curators, would discuss the proposals, and the best approach, if one could call it that, would be the one that gels with the majority. That one would be funded. We see this kind of institute operating everywhere, starting in Africa, to address not just what was looted, but how the communities involved could deal with the consequences of those actions today.

– You have made your thoughts about deconstructing colonial models very clear. But for most of Africa the

colonial era is now past. The future is about new challenges, technology, climate, pandemics. What comes after the decolonisation project?

KK Unfortunately, it is a past and indeed present predisposition that continues to haunt us. With that said, one of our projects, the *Maasai Cow Corridors* in Nairobi, offers a hint at how we look to addressing this history and the present at the same time. We call it the reverse future. For thousands of years the Maasai lived with their cattle, before being displaced by the British colonial administration from their homelands. Today's neoliberalist pressures continue to sideline them. We began to think about an infrastructure that would allow them to come back to the city and maintain that connection, because it is their right as the original keepers of the land. We designed a rainwater-collection reservoir using cave geometry, an oasis where the Maasai could water their cattle and wild animals can find shade and refuge.

This thinking was informed by the urgency of human-induced climate change. At Mount Suswa we are trying to do much the same, with proposals such as VHS (the Volcanic Steam Harvester), that allow people to not only elevate their status but also create a museum environment where people can feel at home. In a nutshell: such projects are born through a thinking of reverse futurism, which intertwines the past into the present and projects into the future using a mix of the two.

SM Extraction is still going on. But now the climate crisis is putting everyone on a more level playing field. For too long, Africa had been playing at the bottom of the slope, so we could never get to the top of the hill. The future is about leaving that behind, so we

are all on a par and decisions are made collectively. At the core of our challenges is the realisation that no one should come to the table with a higher authority or an "I know better than you" attitude. We need to be at the same level. We should discuss and agree, without any coercion.

This text first appeared in:
András Szántó, *Imagining the Future Museum: 21 Dialogues with Architects* (Hatje Cantz, 2022).

András Szántó, Hungarian-born advisor of museums, cultural institutions and leading brands on cultural strategy. An author and editor, his writings have appeared in the *New York Times, Artforum*, the *Art Newspaper* and many other publications. He has overseen the National Arts Journalism Program at Columbia University and the Global Museum Leaders Colloquium at the Metropolitan Museum of Art. Szántó, who lives in Brooklyn, New York, US, has been conducting conversations with art world leaders since the early 1990s, including as a frequent moderator of the Art Basel Conversations series.

Notes

1   Kabage Karanja and Stella Mutegi, "The Anthropocene Museum: Tracing our Decolonial Architectural Movements of Resistance in Africa," *Slow Spatial Reader: Chronicles of Radical Affection*, ed. Carolyn F. Strauss. (Valiz, 2021).

2   Kabage Karanja and Stella Mutegi, "Profile: The Anthropocene Museum: A Troublesome Trail of Improvision Towards the Chthulucene," *Design Studio Vol. 4: Working at the Intersection: Architecture After the Anthropocene*, eds. Harriet Harriss and Naomi House. (Riba Publishing, April 2022).

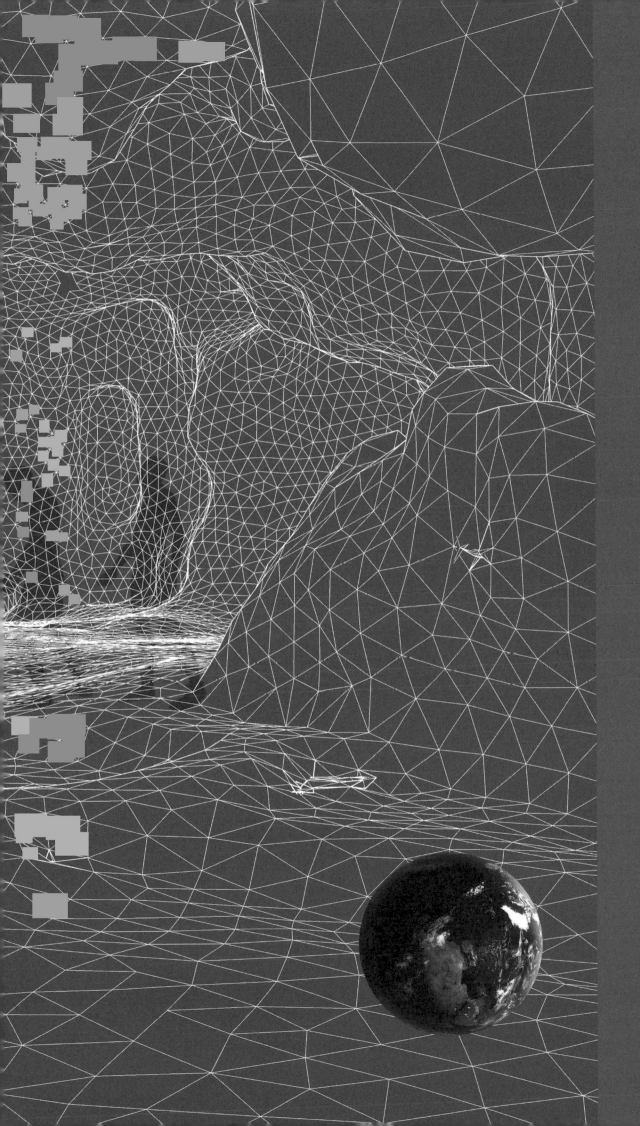

Shimoni Slave Caves

The Anthropocene Museum 2.0

In 2021, we travelled 500 kilometres down to the coastal town of Shimoni in Kwale county which sits on the Indian ocean in Kenya. It is a site that holds the little known Shimoni Slave Caves and the even less known Three Giant Sisters Caves of refuge. In our research we highlight that the world knows quite a lot about the West African Trans-Atlantic slave trade, but very little about what took place on the East African side. Trade from the East African coast is predominantly understood to have been between the Portuguese, the Arabs and the local Indigenous people, but it has also been linked to the British, who continued to exploit enslaved labour after George III signed the Abolition of the Slave Trade Act of 1807.

We spoke with the local custodians of the caves in Shimoni and Twaka, who narrated the dark history that was meted out here. The caves were used as slave holding chambers while a number of the slaves escaped into the vast networks to find refuge in the Three Giant Sisters Caves several kilometres away. Today this connecting corridor has been silted up, leaving archaeological evidence of this past.

The community today imagines a future where they can excavate into the silted networks to uncover evidence of the past and mobilise the disillusioned youth who find it troubling to come to terms with its history. The three-dimensional scans of the cave remain in drawing form and archive awaiting further plans for curation and archaeological exploration to uncover more complex histories within the accumulation of silt and sand.

Anthropocene Museum 2.0: *Shimoni Slave Caves*, Shimoni and Twaka, Kwale County, Kenya, 2021. The World Around Summit, online and in residence at the Solomon R. Guggenheim Museum, New York. Community engagement, short film, exhibition and journal publications ("The Underground," *Architectural Review*, April 2021 issue).

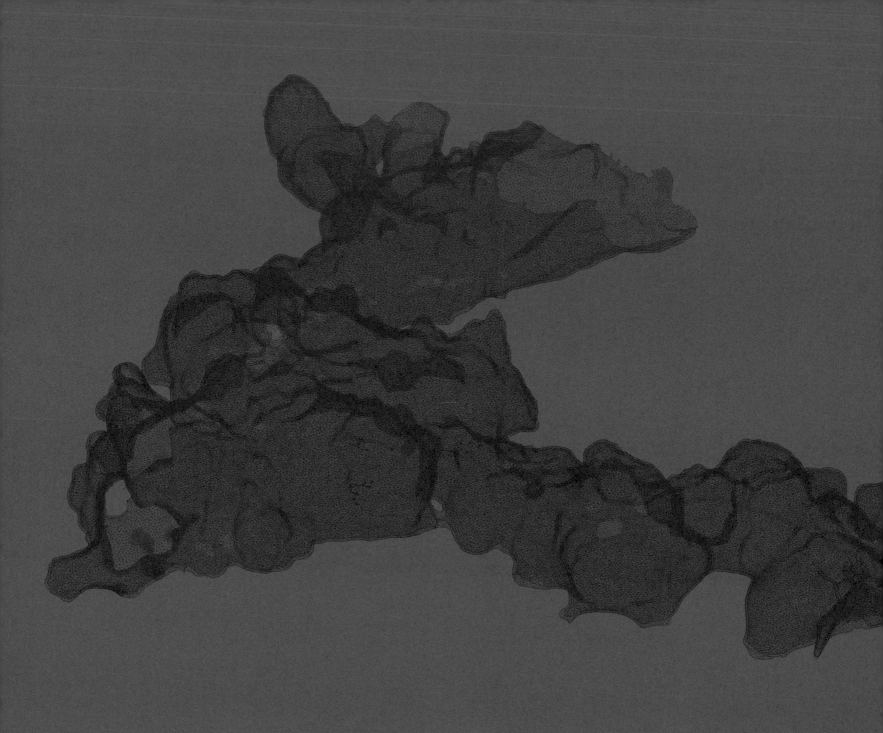

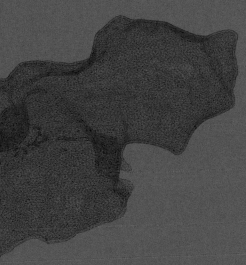

Cave_bureau, 3D scan of Shimoni Slave Caves. Cave_bureau uses 3D scans for research of the spatial qualities of the caves and for reworking into new architectural projects.
Enslaved individuals aboard a slave ship.

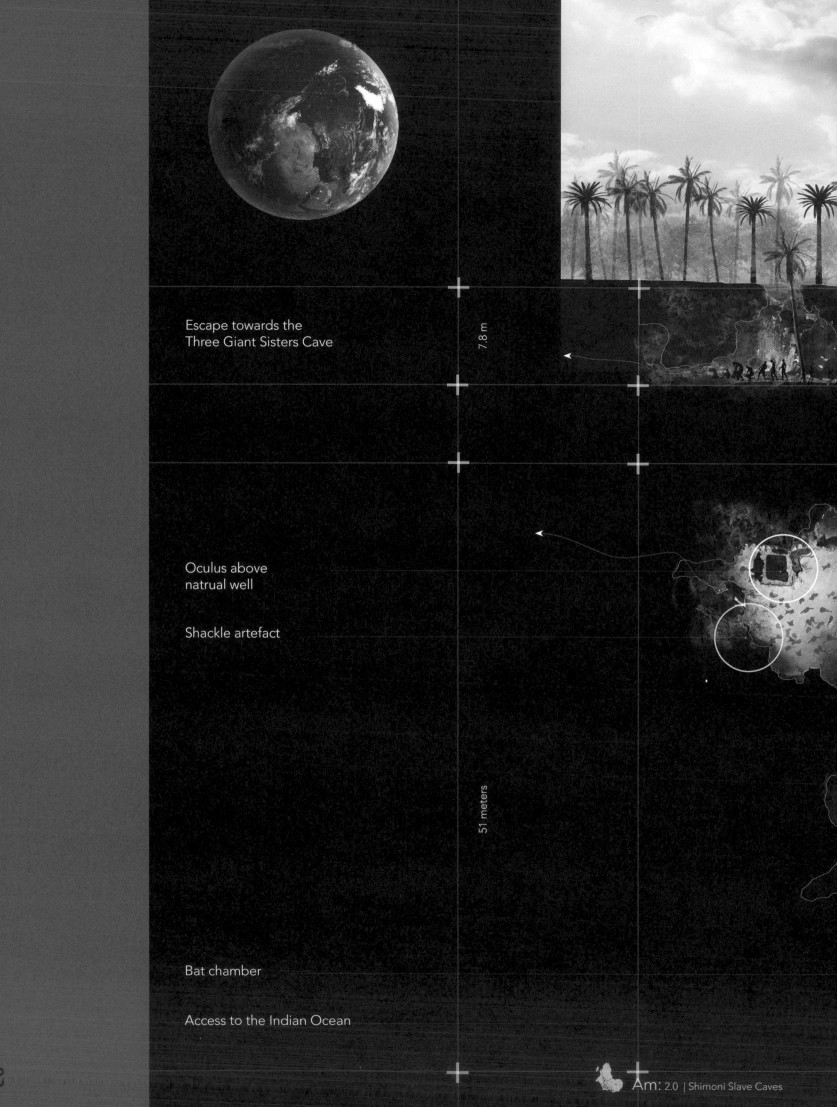

Escape towards the
Three Giant Sisters Cave

7.8 m

Oculus above
natrual well

Shackle artefact

51 meters

Bat chamber

Access to the Indian Ocean

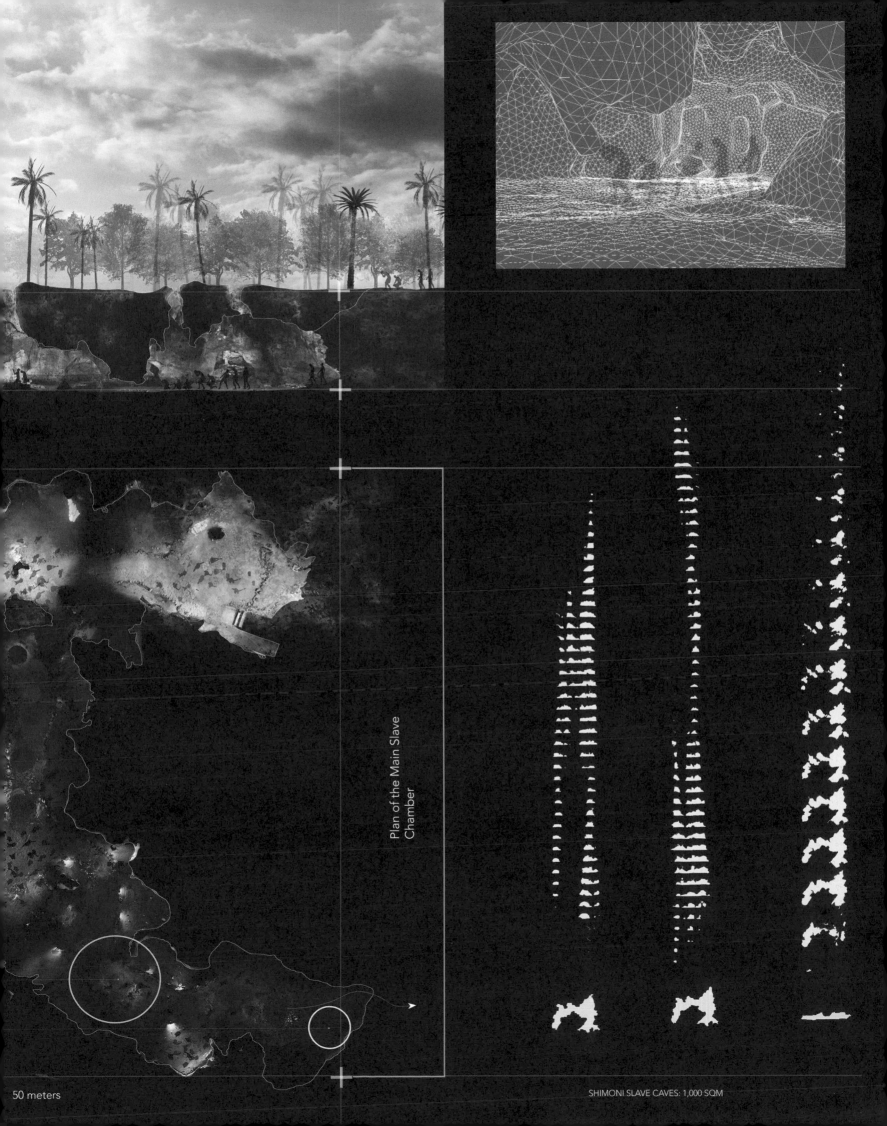

Plan of the Main Slave Chamber

50 meters

SHIMONI SLAVE CAVES: 1,000 SQM

Underground Rivers of the Anthropocene

By Mark Williams, Jan Zalasiewicz and Molly Desorgher

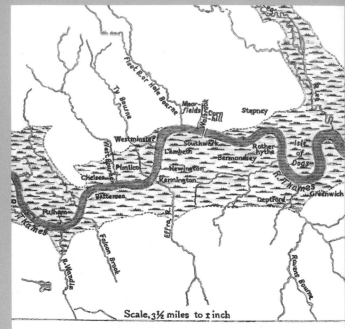

Ancient London and its Surrounding Marshes

The Anthropocene is the time when humanity's collective actions are overwhelming the great forces of nature, to change the course of our planet's history and leave a permanent imprint in Earth's rock strata.[1] In the twenty-first century we move far more sediment than all the world's rivers each year, we have translocated thousands of species beyond their native ranges and we have converted half of all habitable land to agriculture. One part of our colossal impact has been the control of freshwater, now pumped across the Earth in vast quantities and consumed in urban spaces in ways that support neither conservation nor recycling. These patterns of interaction with water are wholly different from those of our ancestors, who lived alongside streams and rivers and often venerated them for their life-giving properties.[2] In the Anthropocene, we are increasingly decoupling rivers from their landscapes by force, so they become polluted, engineered and in many cases completely forgotten. Some no longer flow through the landscape but instead travel in perpetual darkness through human-made underground cave systems. How did cities come to incarcerate the very streams that once provided their lifeblood?

Here we focus on the rivers of London that have been hidden underground (1). Many cities around the world have done the same, and we use the subterranean waters of London[3] as a metaphor for our wider relationship with the Earth, one that signals control and domination in the Anthropocene – albeit a kind of domination that has built-in instability and that therefore may be transient.

Rivers have flowed at the surface of the Earth for billions of years, their paths determined by gravity, landscape, climate and – for the last 400 million years – vegetation. For all that time they inter-acted with many different terrains, flowing faster across steep ground and slower where the incline is gentler. Gradually they wore down high mountains, cut deep valleys and carved out wide floodplains. In some places they shaped underground canyons too, through soluble rocks such as limestone. As they flowed, they carried sediment and nutrients across the land and to the oceans, and thus have been an integral part of Earth's life-support system. On the land itself, the flow of rivers interacts intimately with life. Woodlands, meadows and

marshes help direct the river's meanders across its floodplain. These patterns of loops and bends formed good places for human civilisation to develop, providing a supply of water, a safe place to build a harbour, a means of connecting with the outside world. On one such bend of the River Thames, a small city began to flourish, two thousand years ago. This early Roman settlement would later become London. At its start it was small and vulnerable, just a few thousand people, but it was already modifying the river system, building quays along the northern bank of the Thames, and constructing the first bridge across it (2).

Roman London secured its water supply within its bounds, walling in the downstream portion of a small freshwater stream that would later become known as the Walbrook. The stream flowed through the heart of the settlement (2). No written accounts of how the city's early inhabitants related to the Walbrook are left, but archaeological evidence shows that its banks were raised to compensate for flooding,[4] and that the downstream floodplain was already accumulating waste from the city. In the third century CE, a temple to the Roman god Mithras was built on its eastern bank, and other archaeological remains within that river's ancient course suggest some mystical attachment with the local people.[5] Much later, as the modern city developed, the Walbrook became polluted and was then entombed,[6] its waters eventually co-opted into London's sewer system. It had already disappeared from the surface by the time the first map of London was made in the middle of the sixteenth century (3) (the preceding spread). Interred beneath the city, the Walbrook's ancient course runs beneath the Bank of England, its memory recalled only by a nearby street that bears its name.

From mythical rivers to super sewer

The Walbrook is not the only one of London's rivers to have been imprisoned. Upstream along the Thames to the west of Roman London was a larger river. Like the Walbrook, its Roman (and perhaps earlier Celtic) name is lost, but later it would come to be known as the Fleet, an Anglo-Saxon name meaning tidal inlet.[7] Rising in the higher ground on Hampstead Heath in north London, this river's

valley seems to have provided water for the Anglo-Saxon people who settled in early medieval London, with many springs and wells, some thought to have healing properties. Despite the Fleet's importance as a source of freshwater, it fared no better than the Walbrook. By the seventeenth century its waters were being used as an open sewer. It survived as a heavily engineered 'river' above ground until the nineteenth century.[8] Thereafter it vanished, subsumed into the underground sewer network (4), its name to survive in Fleet Street, once home of the newspaper industry in London.

The physical imprisonment of the Walbrook and Fleet echo London's growing domination of its landscape as the modern city evolved. Below the ground, the ancient rivers were co-opted to carry away the city's waste, while above the ground the physical and spiritual connections between London's rivers and its inhabitants were severed. Rivers of water were obscured by rivers of money, as capital flowed through the city's banks, and by flotillas of goods too, as trade grew. This pattern of domination was repeated across the city. The eleven kilometre stretch of the River Tyburn was repurposed for the sewer system, as was, on the south bank of the Thames, the River Effra[9]: its entry to the Thames flows beneath the headquarters of MI6, the Secret Intelligence Service made famous by the fictitious spy, James Bond.

While most of London's rivers flow beneath the city, one seems to defy gravity above ground. This is the Westbourne, which for a short part of its journey flows through the middle of Sloane Square metro station, carried by a large cast-iron pipe above the train track.[10] In the past, its waters were used for drinking, but the spread of London's flushable toilets in the nineteenth century soured its flow. No longer able to shape the landscape around it, the Westbourne's waters make way for the daily flow of commuters that ride the underground trains of London. And, as with the trains, much of the flow of London's underground rivers is driven by fossil fuels rather than by gravity, via the pumping stations that now force and guide the flow.

Thus, by the late nineteenth century, London had engineered, constrained, buried and redirected most of the tributary rivers that fed into the Thames. No longer allowed to flow naturally, they act now as a network of sewers. They carry away human waste to be cleansed, and artificially cleaned water is returned to the above-ground river system. And so, the city comes to resemble one super-organism, its flows of energy arriving from all quarters of the Earth, its people carried through underground burrows that criss-cross the major transport hubs and beyond. Its manufactured goods are dispersed along the river to the world, its waste disposed of through a complex subterranean gut. As the city grew wider and doubled in size between the nineteenth and twentieth centuries, new rivers began to flow below ground. The many kilometres of the Thames Water Ring Main are hidden tens of metres below London. It is the source of much of the water that courses through countless homes, flowing in a stop-start motion when taps are turned on and off or toilets flushed. In this way, the Ring Main carries thousands of millions of litres of water a day.[11] And, as the Victorian sewer system gradually became overwhelmed, yet another subterranean river grew, to become the concrete pipes that are known as London's 'Super Sewer.'[12]

While the ancient rivers still flow, albeit underground, their invisibility renders them mostly forgotten in favour of more visible, profitable flows – for instance those of capital, power, people, goods and information – forming part of a yet larger system that now binds all of humanity and its technology into the planet-spanning techno-sphere.[13] The notion of a technosphere has been developed by the American scientist Peter Haff. It comprises our industrial, agricul-tural, transport, communications, power and financial systems; our interconnected bureaucracies and social systems; our military and educational facilities. We humans are bound within it, and now depend on it to stay alive. It is a system with its own emergent dy-namics that is growing rapidly in its complexity and mass.[14] Like the other great spheres of the Earth – of earth, water, air and life – the technosphere can be found everywhere at its surface and in many cases under the ground. It is a driving force of the Anthropocene, ever-increasing in its total mass, its influence, the rate at which it turns resources into waste and in its ability to overwhelm the Earth.

Unlike the other spheres, which have interacted over billions

of years to create a habitable Earth,[15] the technosphere has grown in a geological 'eyeblink' to become a voracious consumer, one that gives back very little of what it takes. It is in cities that most of the technosphere's consumption takes place. It is here that most human energy is consumed, that most of our waste is generated and – since the beginning of the twenty-first century – where most people live.[16] The disappearance, by internment, of London's rivers in turn makes visible the city's change of relationship with its environment into one of increasing domination, control and exploitation. No longer dependent on its local tributaries for a supply of freshwater, the city first converted them to open toilets and then buried them underground. Only the mighty Thames and its western tributary the Lea withstood this onslaught, as they alone continued to provide the technosphere with a means to transport its materials, and a continued source of water – once treated – to sustain its co-opted humans.

Daylight is coming to the technosphere

London is not alone in devouring its rivers. In Sydney, Australia, the city's roots were founded on a small freshwater creek called the Tank Stream,[17] which centuries ago may have been a supply of freshwater and fish for the Indigenous Gadigal people. Within a few decades of Europeans arriving, the river was little more than an open sewer, which then became a buried sewer, and then a storm drain (5). On the other side of the world, 16,000 kilometres away from Sydney, the rivers of New York City fared no better. The ancient river Mosholu – renamed Tibbets Brook – is one of these. Its Algonquin name means "smooth stones," and for generations it was likely a source of fresh water and food for the Lenape people.[18] It was first overprinted with the name of the British settler George Tibbetts in the seventeenth century, and then physically buried by the city itself – it was dammed, diverted and then, in the middle of the twentieth century, culverted. As a final step, the brook became a receptacle for raw sewage from illegal drain connections.[19] On every continent where people live in cities, rivers have vanished, subsumed into underground sewer systems.

Still, some cities seek to make amends by bringing their hidden

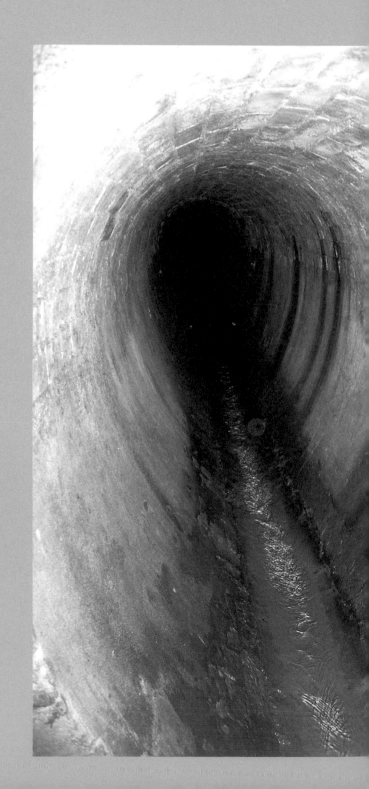

rivers back into daylight.[20] New York plans to return at least part of Mosholu to the surface after a century of darkness, along with enhancing the local ecosystem around the Van Cortlandt Lake, which was produced by damming Tibbets Brook in the eighteenth century.[21] Today, buried streams like Tibbets Brook sometimes reappear as flood-waters above ground during heavy rainfall and storms.[22] It is hoped that the 'daylighting' of rivers may help to reduce the flood risk, restore urban river ecologies, reduce strain on sewer systems and even help cities cope with climate change in places where rainfall will increase. Some individuals have also taken direct action to make a city's rivers clean again. In East London the River Roding flows into the Thames at Barking. It is polluted upstream from farmland agricultural run-off, and downstream from sewer overflows. But it has a human champion, one who seeks to reconnect the river with the city's inhabitants, and to take on those in authority who do nothing to protect its flow.[23] These small efforts, if they can grow, might seek to alleviate and counter some of the damage caused by the growth of the technosphere, by restoring and reconnecting urban riverine ecosystems.

The technosphere is a new phenomenon, but if we collectively remain indifferent to our actions, it may be short-lived. Unless we can help steer it towards a more sympathetic relationship to the natural world, it is destined to be crippled by its appetite for Earth's resources and suffocated by its own waste. Just now and then, when London's underground rivers become inundated with heavy rain, they break through at the surface, to remind Londoners they still exist, and to signal what may come if the technosphere ceases to function. It is almost as if they say: Imagine when the technosphere's flows of capital stop, the central power of the city fades, its transportation systems fail. Then, the brick-built and concrete culverts will decay, abraded and rotted by the minerals and sediments that flow within the water, just as rivers have cut their courses for millennia. The underground rivers will be released as the pumping stations fail and the city above them begins to collapse. At the surface, the River Thames will continue rolling onwards to the sea, slowly shaking off the brick and concrete corset that fixed it in place for centuries. On the higher ground, to the north and south of that river, small streams will begin to flow again, eventually coalescing with the Tyburn, Westbourne, Fleet, Walbrook and Effra as these are freed again from the sewer system.

As time passes, and London's buildings are pulled apart by the wind and the rain, the river valley becomes a deciduous woodland again. The Earth's natural connections between air, earth, life and water reassert themselves, and maintain a habitable place for life here that continues millions of years into the future. Unimpeded, the rivers of London begin to flow again through a rich habitat of beech, ash, oak and alder, their waters ever sweeter as toxins are flushed away. Hedgehogs, foxes and otter reclaim the landscape. The technosphere here has gone, and so too have most – or all – of its humans. Beneath the ground, the collapsed concrete tunnels and brick-lined culverts gradually fill with sediment, eventually to become the gigantic, fossilised remains of the subterranean city and of the technosphere. They have grown as monstrous versions of what geologists call bioturbation in ancient strata: the tracks left by burrowing and crawling animals. These enormous structures will include the complex traceries of metal left by pipes and wires, plastic debris of all kinds, scatterings of ceramic tiles, decaying machinery – and perhaps even the remains of some of the last human inhabitants of the city, as they used these unnatural cave systems for shelter. Long into the future – perhaps millions of years hence – these can persist, until they are revealed by erosion. Perhaps they will be visited by future archaeologists who, assembling the artefacts contained within them, may wonder how, and why, such vast, unsustainable and unsympathetic structures were ever built.

Notes

1 Julia Adeney Thomas, Mark Williams and Jan Zalasiewicz, *The Anthropocene: A Multidisciplinary Approach* (Polity Books, 2020).

2 Larry W. Mays and Andreas N. Angelicas, Demetris Koutsoyiannis, Nikos Mamassis, "Ancient Gods and Goddesses of Water," *Evolution of Water Supply Throughout the Millennia* (IWA Publishing, 2012).

3 Andy Dangerfield, "The lost rivers that lie beneath London," BBC News, 4 October 2015.

4 Stephen D. Myers, "The River Walbrook and Roman London," PhD thesis (University of Reading, 2016), https://centaur.reading.ac.uk 68935/1/19021540_Myers_thesis.pdf.

5 Fiona Rule, *London's Docklands: A History of the Lost Quarter* (The History Press, 2019), 384.

6 Derek Keene, "Issues of water in medieval London to c. 1300," *Urban History 28*, no. 2 (August 2001), 161-179.

7 Bill McCann and Clive Orton, "The Fleet Valley Project," *London Archaeologist 6*, (1989), 102-107.

8 *The History of the River Fleet*, compiled by the University College London Fleet Restoration Team, 2009, https:// www.camden.gov.uk/documents/20142/1458280/River+Fleet.pdf/0f0063cc-7079-32c2-5822-6306dcd56d62.

9 Bradley L Garrett, "Picturing Urban Subterranea: Embodied Aesthetics of London's Sewers," *Environment and Planning A 48*, no. 10, (October 2016), 1948-1966.

10 Paul Talling, *London's Lost Rivers* (Random House, 2011), 190.

11 "London Ring Main turns 25," Thames Water (November 2019), https://www.thameswater.co.uk/about-us/newsroom/latest-news/2019/nov/london-ring-main-turnstwenty- five.

12 "Thames Tideway Tunnel," Thames Water, https://www.thameswater.co.uk/aboutus/investing-in-our-region/thames-tideway-tunnel.

13 Peter K. Haff, "Technology asa Geological Phenomenon: Implications for Human Wellbeing," *A Stratigraphical Basis for the Anthropocene* (Geological Society London,

Special Publication 395, 2014), 301-309.

14 Jan Zalasiewicz, "The Unbearable Burden of the Technosphere," UNESCO Courier 2 (2018), https://en.unesco.org/courier/2018-2/unbearableburden-technosphere.

15 Mark Williams and Jan Zalasiewicz, *The Cosmic Oasis: The Remarkable Story of Earth's Biosphere* (Oxford University Press, 2022).

16 Mark Williams, Julia Thomas, Gavin Brown, Minal Pathak, Moya Burns, Will Steffen, John Clarkson and Jan Zalasiewicz, "Mutualistic Cities of the Near Future," *Altered Earth*, ed. J.A. Thomas (Cambridge University Press, 2022).

17 "The Tank Stream," Sydney Water, https://www.sydneywater.com.au/content/dam/sydneywater/documents/tankstreamheritage-fact-sheet.pdf.

18 NYC Parks, https://www.nycgovparks.org/parks/VanCortlandtPark/highlights/8183.

19 Storch Associates, *Restoration Master Plan*, (New York City Parks Department, 1986), https://smedia.nyc.gov/agencies/lpc/arch_reports/98_B.pdf, and https://s-media.nyc.gov/agencies/lpc/arch_reports/98_A.pdf.

20 David N. Lerner, "Many Urban Rivers are Hidden Underground – 'Daylighting' Them Would Bring Nature Back to Cities," The Conversation, 2019, https://theconversation.com/manyurban-rivers-are-hiddenunderground-daylightingthem-would-bring-natureback-to-cities-128441.

21 Tibbets Brook Daylighting Project, https://www.nyc.gov/site/dep/whats-new/tibbetts-brook-daylightingproject.page.

22 Winnie Hu and James Thomas, "Why New York Is Unearthing a Brook It Buried a Century Ago," *New York Times*, December 2021.

23 Patrick Barkham: "'The Roding is sacred and has rights': the hammer-wielding barrister fighting for London's forgotten river," *The Guardian*, December 2022.

Molly Desorgher is an Anthropocene geographer, wild swimmer, sailor and PhD student at the University of Leicester, UK. Their research takes an interscalar, multidisciplinary approach to understanding the processes by which the technosphere constructs (seemingly) impermeable boundaries between people and waterways, in order to find cracks in these constructions through which entanglement and interpermeation might seep.

Mark Williams is a palaeontologist and professor of palaeobiology at the University of Leicester, UK. He is interested in the history of life on Earth, has it evolved over billions of years. Most recently, he has focussed on the human impact on life in the Anthropocene, with cities and their waterways being a major component of that impact. He is a long-time member of the Anthropocene Working Group and a co-author of several popular science books with his friend Jan Zalasiewicz.

Jan Zalasiewicz is professor emeritus of palaeobiology at the University of Leicester, UK. He chairs the Subcommission on Quaternary Stratigraphy and is part of its Anthropocene Working Group. His interests include Early Palaeozoic fossils and rocks, the Quaternary Ice Ages and the geology made by humans. His books include *The Earth After Us* (2008), *The Planet in a Pebble* (2010) and (with Mark Williams) *The Goldilocks Planet* (2012), *Ocean Worlds* (2014), *Skeletons* (2018) and *The Cosmic Oasis* (2022), all published by Oxford University Press.

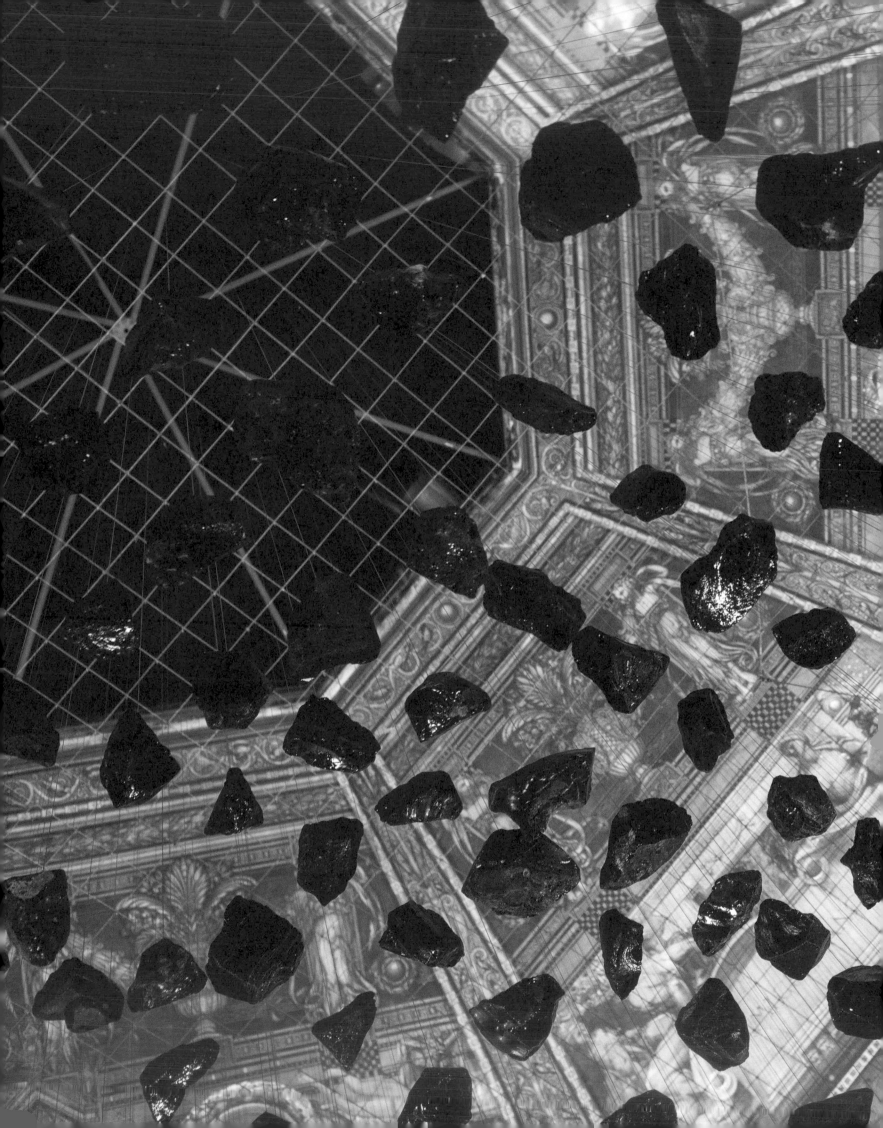

Obsidian
Rain

The Anthropocene Museum 3.0

As invited participants of the 17th Venice Biennale of Architecture in 2021, we transposed a 1:1 hanging installation of the Mau Mau Freedom Fighters Cave within the Giardini Galileo Chinioctagonal dome. Here we imagined patrons of the exhibition entering the central pavilion to have a shared experience of the cave roof of 1,680 hanging obsidian stones lowered to the same cloud levels taken from the decolonial Mbai Cave that we scanned almost six years earlier. This cave was used by the Mau Mau to not only find refuge, but as a place to imagine an African state of the future, and as a site to orchestrate the resistance.

On the exhibition floor were two steel tables of 1:100 bronze models of the Mbai Cave, one sliced horizontally in plan to reveal the hanging section, while the other fully intact. A hybrid of leather printed drawings hung from the edges of the cave. Across the floor were salvaged tree stumps for visitors to linger and look up and reflect on our collective architectural heritage and legacy of trauma. The cave was structurally supported using hexagonal laminate veneer lumber from the forests of Mensa in Finland that were recycled for other projects after the exhibition. Our question was, how will we live together when our recent colonial histories of oppression, extermination and erasure are still left open ended and not being redressed for past and future generations to register?

Anthropocene Museum 3.0: *Obsidian Rain*. Mbai Caves, Nairobi, Kiambu County, Nairobi, Kenya and the 17th Venice Biennale of Architecture, 2021. Exhibition, installation, bronze models, leather drawings, newspaper publication (*New York Times* online).

cave

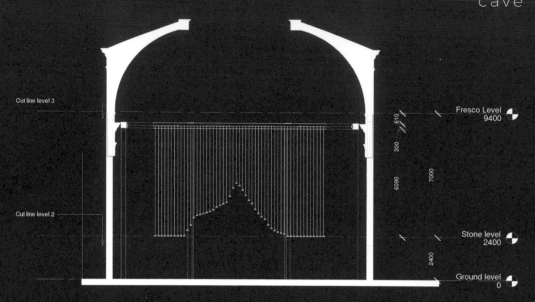

Cut line level 3

Cut line level 2

Fresco Level
9400

Stone level
2400

Ground level
0

3 Grid 1 Copy 1
1 : 100

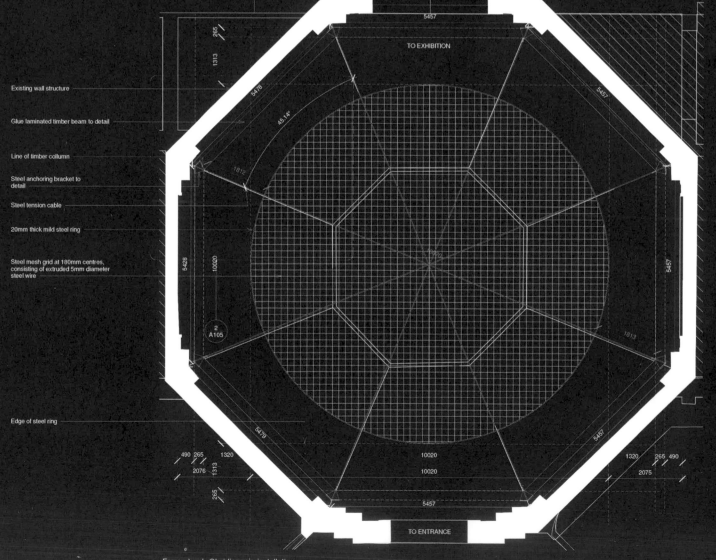

Existing wall structure

Glue laminated timber beam to detail

Line of timber collumn

Steel anchoring bracket to detail

Steel tension cable

20mm thick mild steel ring

Steel mesh grid at 180mm centres, consisting of extruded 5mm diameter steel wire

Edge of steel ring

TO EXHIBITION

45.14°

TO ENTRANCE

1 Fresco level- Obsidian rain installation
1 : 50

Mbai Cave, Kenya. Obsidian, found in abundance in the Great Rift Valley, is an igneous rock occurring as a natural glass, formed by the rapid cooling of viscous lava from volcanoes. Cave_bureau worked on this rock that caused cuts to their hands, just like it once did to their ancestors' hands. A return to the birth place of their technological heritage, where it all began.

Cow Corridor

The Anthropocene Museum 4.0

The Maasai people were the first inhabitants of Nairobi city, which they called Enkare Nyrobi meaning 'the place of cool waters.' In discussion with two Maasai women, Dorcas Sasine and Emily Lankenua, who live on the outskirts of Nairobi, we developed a vision of a time when the Maasai would be allowed to herd their cattle through Nairobi, on their ancestral lands, without being harassed or arrested – a remnant of past colonial city bylaws. This project is built on a resistance of the anthropogenic histories of imperialism and colonialism in Kenya that has dislocated people from the natural systems and processes on earth to the detriment of the majority of city dwellers.

From an architectural perspective, as Edward Ihejirika (chief inspector and director of education of Midwestern Nigeria) has said, the modern movement denied the primacy of language and representation, reinforcing the colonial project through the international style. The *Cow Corridor* presents a counter-reality to address these states of dysfunction and imposed urbanism through what we call a remedial act of reverse futurism. The project provides an urban infrastructure where the Maasai can graze their cows in the city, which includes a network of routes intertwined with tourist pathways, designated grazing zones, watering holes, salt licks, veterinary clinics and Maasai market trading zones.

The shade foliage and rainwater collectors are developed using the reversed geometries of the Shimoni Slave Caves. Here we contemplate the theoretical and practical return of our species to an origin that is and always was beyond carbon neutral. To realise this project we propose the establishing of the Benevolent Reparations Institute, an imagined institution in the making, fuelled to creatively attract the return of stolen wealth to the arts for peoples of the Global South, without total reliance on the Global North's waning guilt.

Anthropocene Museum 4.0: *Cow Corridor*, Nairobi, Kenya, 2021. Written manifesto, online publication (Dezeen)

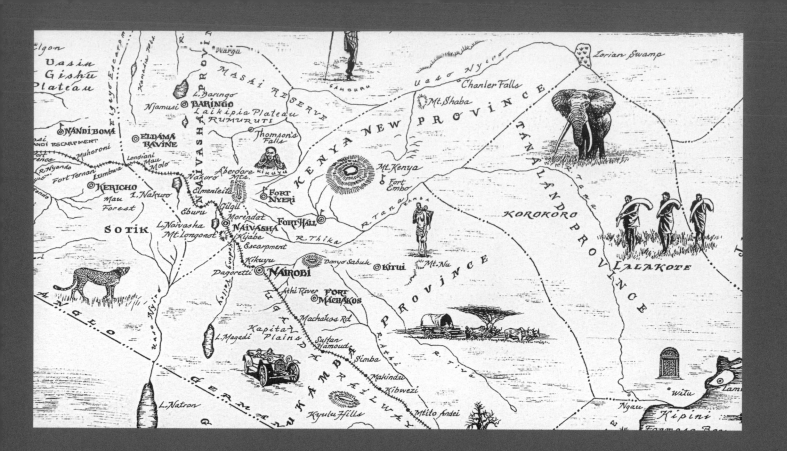

Map of Kenya and surrounding countries during the British settler occupation and colonisation. Still today, the subdivision of land and creation of plantations makes it impossible for the Maasai to graze their cattle and live their rich free-range, pastoral life. There is a hundred years between the two photos of the British farmer and the Maasai cow herd.

Prehistoric rock paintings in Manda Guéli Cave in the Ennedi Mountains, Chad.
The discussions between Cave_bureau and the Maasai women Dorcas Sasine and Emily Lankenua
nourished the ideas for the *Cow Corridor*.

Cave_bureau, *Cow Corridor* collages. The *Cow Corridor* is intended to stretch from the Jomo Kenyatta International Airport reserve land, right into Nairobi's derelict railway yards, underutilised road reserves and riparian areas.

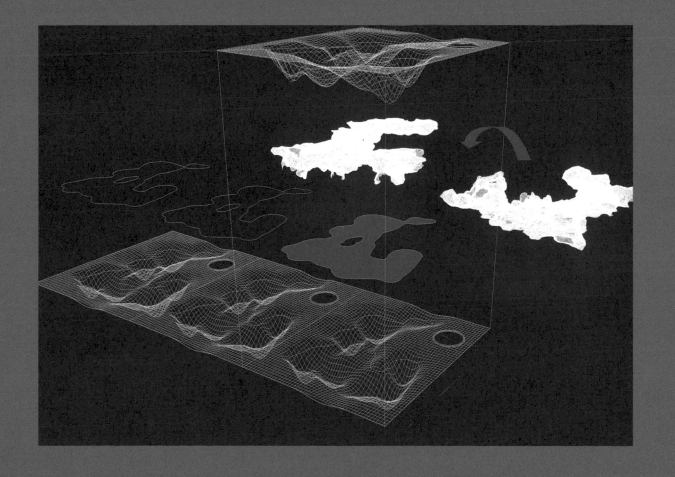

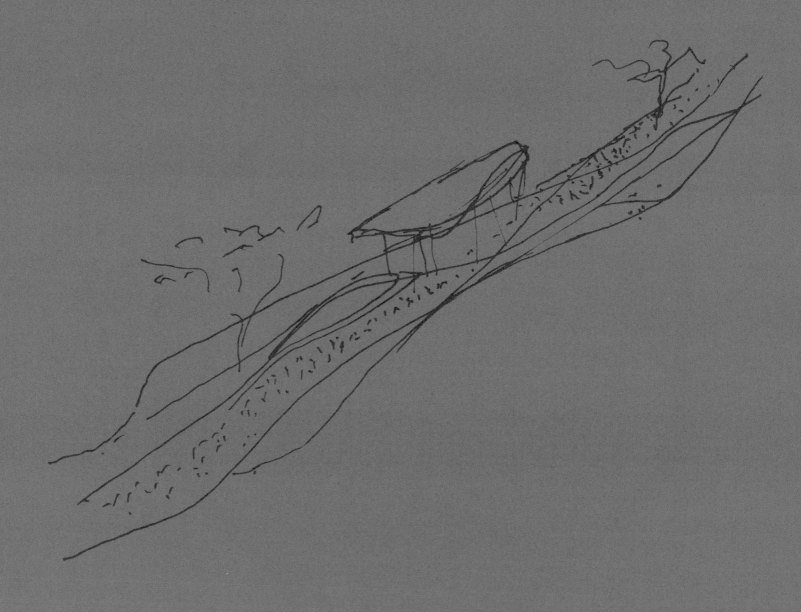

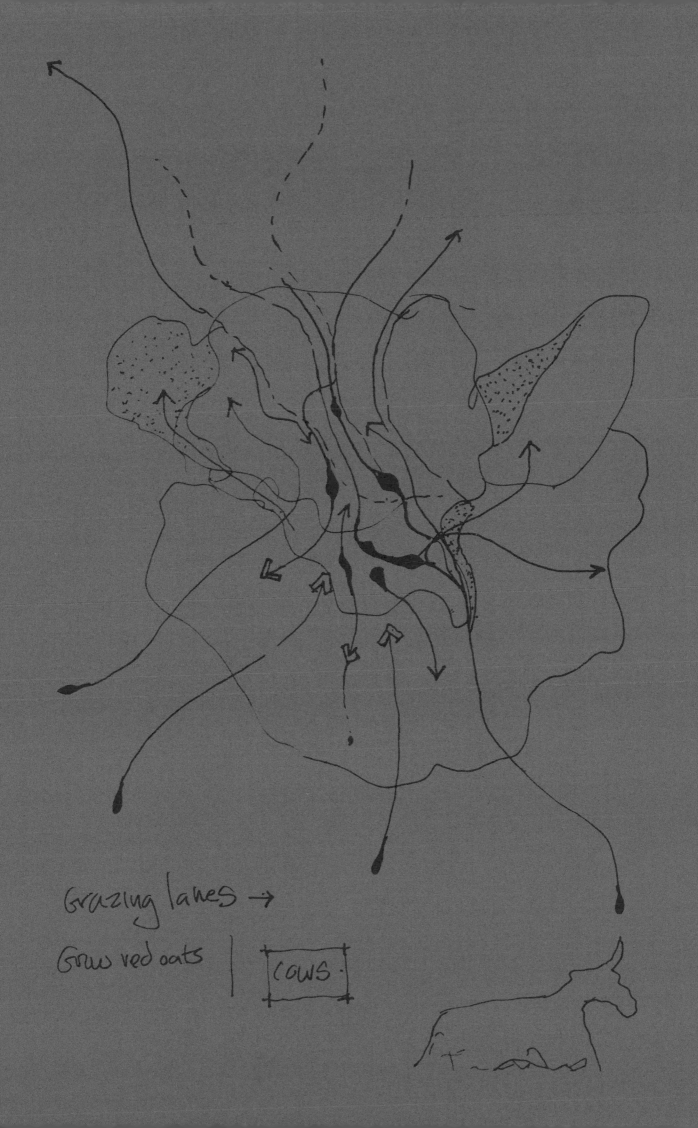

Grazing lanes →

Grow red oats | COWS.

Cave_bureau, *Cow Corridor* collage. The *Cow Corridor* shade foliage and rainwater collectors are developed using reversed geometries of the Shimoni Slave Caves of Kwale

Ancestral Urbanisms of the Anthropocene

By Kathryn Yusoff

Given that the Anthropocene designates a planetary epoch of geologic change, questions of scale and participation are newly raised in architecture – architecture understood as a geographical practice of coherencies towards or contra to the praxis of colonial earth that has built this new geologic state. Where does architecture begin and end if the earth has been geoengineered through colonial materialism and its processes into a made earth?

The Anthropocene is a particular geosocial material arrangement of colonialism and extraction that modifies the Earth through the praxis of race, resulting in the marginalisation of the racialised poor. What is the cost of architectural forms that continue to propagate the myth of architecture as materially isolated from the mine and the memory of life-worlds that prior materialisms held in place.

Architecture's approach within the genre of natural resources has often been to produce a language of materiality that is independent of its former earth attachments and location. Indeed, architecture is the genre by which the transformation of a placed-based material world becomes one in which place is created anew, often with materials severed from the life-worlds it sustained elsewhere.

The Anthropocene materially raises the question of how to live with undergrounds and un-grounded peoples (who have been displaced or violently dissuaded from their attachment to the ground by dominant colonial or neoliberal forces).

Cave_bureau directly engages this social and geologic origin story of what colonialism made. The erasure of undergrounds, above and below ground (both as labour and materials), which service surface architectures and urban centres establish a geologic infrastructure that expands spatial values dictated by colonial models of extraction and expansion. While class might take over as a socio-economic differentiator in the maintenance of spatial differentiation established by colonial racial apartheids, the actual underground has a parallel in architectural practices that seek to erase the context of materiality and maintain its independence from its geographical and geological circumstances of the unseen labour and earth that makes it.

While attention is often drawn to the 75,000-year-old markings in Blombos Cave in South Africa as part of the cradle of humanity's story, the in-humanism of the Shimoni Caves that Cave_bureau works with gives a different history of the story 'Out of Africa' to the anthropological one that holds Africa in a primal imagination. The 'Out of Africa' prehistoric symbolism of hominid evolution emerges precisely because of colonial activities and becomes part of a narrative that normalises and naturalises the colonialisation of the earth. On the way to homo sapiens' dispersal and migration to the West, 'Out of Africa' was read as prehistory to colonial history, which was narrated as *the* arrival of that evolutionary arc in the West. Theorists of human origins, overdetermined the telos of a singular migratory force to justify colonialism's extinctions. The always present origin story, of various 'Out of Africas', repeated in the collective sense, is a processual habituation of colonial powers in making Africa 'birth' but not future, origin but not end. Making Africa resource but not resourceful.

There is a kind of Africa-genesis in colonial lives and afterlives that constantly flatten and figurately 'past' the African present in either the axis of origins or the promissory futurity of development in various forms of 'Africa rising'. From what? We might ask. Global discourses imagine Africa rising, as if it had somehow been in a depressed swamp rather than in the grip of trade that is organised around extraction, neocolonial corruption and models of geography that organise racial deficits that see wealth disproportionally taken 'off continent'.

The long-time colonial story of material determinism has been that Africa will rise when she exploits all her natural resources. And cities are a key site in the development of the trade in colonial minerals. 'Out of Africa' faster than the value. Leave the bedrock and float on up through multinationals to another stock exchange in London or New York. 'Out of Africa' imagined as escape: minerals and metals on their way to the London Metal Exchange; skulls tagged as anthropological spoil to the British Museum to furnish a scientific reputation; resources to the Western (and increasingly Chinese) markets. 'Out of Africa' is for the generation of value elsewhere. The racial to mineral deficit model results in a recursive weaponisation of geology for the perseverance of the extraction of value. 'Out of Africa' holds the condition of depletion. Africa in this imagination is always somehow on the move either economically to enrich Western trade or as racialised 'bodies' that threaten geopolitical borders. Academics pen articles on the 'hustle' economy, 'scamming' and sometimes the reparative repair of informal practices of reparations.

The American hip-hop band N.W.A.'s "Straight outta Compton" is the trans-Atlantic return of 'straight outta Africa', understood as a badge of honour in the afterlives of slavery, and often deployed as a contemporary racist dog-whistle. 'Out of Africa' is most definitely not imagined through the small boats and their uncertain passage through the waves and onto British beaches. Cave_bureau's Anthropocene Museums and community practice take on the coloniality of these archetypal colonial imaginaries and their forms of African-genesis — an origination made from outside — to interrupt and install new origins of African futures.

Caves are a gaze from within
The Jamaican cultural theorist Sylvia Wynter (born 1928) says that materially and symbolically, "Blombos Cave reveals the ritual-initiatory transformation of the biologically born individual subject into that of a now fictively-chartered and encoded, thereby, hybrid, bios/mythos autopoietic form of symbolic life."[1] This 'hybrid bio/mythos' form of humanism describes a subject able to both create and narrate itself, through evolution and cultural practices.

The discovery of the caves is for Wynter the actuality of poesies and signifies the human as a storytelling animal, the human is 'homo narrans'.[2] Wynter characterises this as the third origin in cosmic history, after the origins of the universe and the origins of Life. Yet I can't help feeling that Wynter's framing overstates the *bios* and over-reads the significance of the transformation of the human in a hybrid bios-mythos existence, independent of the walls of the cave. What if the *geos* as cave is *the* mutable ground of transformation where/among/through which inscription and narration takes place, rather than a background for this occurrence? What if we think alongside Cave_bureau that the cave is the paradigmatic structure of beginnings, a site in the formation of a geologic subjectivity that expresses a continued relation with this first architecture? Then the *bios* is never dangerously separated from the material origins that precede it.

The cave is not an architectural void or a clean modernist vacuum. Narration takes place with minerals and rocks (oche, particularly, on rock). Narration is in conversation with the durational materiality of the world and its temporal occasions. The inhuman lends a deep-time future that biology does not. Caves are a gaze from within, not necessarily a gaze below, nor above, but within geologically conversant architectures of emergence. As the architects behind Cave_bureau narrate and visualise, their "work addresses the anthropological and geological context of the postcolonial African city as a means to confront the challenges of our contemporary rural and urban lives."[3] Thinking with origin spaces rather than origin stories draws attention to the *actual* material spaces of transformation. And it offers a site for the intervention and transformation of those origin spaces into future architectures.

The human subject is an alterable-architectural subject whose affectual and geological infrastructures we should take seriously as a conditional state of becoming and one that is constantly being differentiated by (post)colonial forces in geopolitics of being. Without erasing those differences, we can also say that we are subjects of geology and that many exalted practices have forgotten that geology is the condition of the emergence of the *bios* (and its forms of narration).

A biopolitical or a narrow geopolitical reading of the subject inverts and thus obscures this environmental context of being, and yet it is the most important thing for the possibility of survival. Orgins are always narration and never nature, but geophysical spaces outlast and are in tension with those narrations and their physical manifestations as architecture. As affectual, material and otherwise infrastructural architectures of inhabitation, caves speak to and with different spatial narratives and moments.

We have the capacity to narrate geography and space differently, and the inhuman may well be a key collaborator in the imagination of that process. Cave_bureau curates caves of resistance against neoliberalist development of geothermal energy extraction that fails to consider or listen to accounts of the local Maasai community in Kenya. Their curation connects temporal inhabitations that proceed and might outlast development as a spatial practice of intervention, suggesting durational architectures to retool environmentally destructive processes.

Thinking the 'cave as museum' addresses moments of cultural, political and historical cave inhabitation, as well as prehistoric originations that organised much longer heritages than the geologically recent histories that have neglected these underground architectures with their surface focus. Thinking about and with underground spaces is also implicated in the larger dynamic of how colonial earth was built. It is a way of thinking with the undergrounds of racial capital or the negative spaces that build what is above ground, while often geographically or socially remote from those sites of extraction.

Urbanisation is a process of drawing people and materials towards often elevated or flow architectures that bifurcate, dwarf or congest around geographical centring. The below ground sites of mines, quarries and undergrounds that bring the architectures of the vertical city into being are elsewhere. Here, we can see architecture as being located in a didactic relation with extraction, where what is built and what is extracted are spatially remote from one another. As the city goes up it also flattens lives and material structures, through forms of precarity and in waves of displacement and disillusion. The city must go up to be recognised as such.

Cave_bureau calls this displacement the 'voids' in the 'made'. The made are the desired urban architectures, and the voids are their margins and spaces of exclusion, existing everywhere there is the made. Rather than thinking from the made to the void as a captive project that provides a promissory inclusion into neoliberal projects founded on exclusion, thinking with the voids to remake the made is a route to a more liberatory ecological futurism. One that is not built on perpetuating the marginalisation and enforced poverty of the made. In my own work, I have been thinking about the differences between these two states – which I call the 'plateau' and the 'rift' – as geophysical spatialities.[4]

I understand the relations between different geologic spatialities as being bound by histories of unequal geo-trauma and geoaccummulation, and experienced in the present as a set of racialised geophysical forces that act to differentiate persons and places, often within the same geographical space. Cave_bureau calls this attention to the voids a 'reverse futurism', a way of making pathways of healing in the midst of colonial and on-going neocolonial affective and administrative architectures.

Imagination can heal colonial geotrauma

The Martinique poet and politician, Aimé Césaire (1913-2008), called for the creation of museums of 'nonnatural history', for all the histories that were made outside of colonial historicising and its pronouncements of a singular universal history of 'Man', which designated Europe and the West as the apex and the narrative police of that historicising. These museums of nonnatural history would gather all the erased and discarded histories and through them tell the stories of the forgotten.

Césaire argued in his *Discourse on Colonialism* (1950) that colonists used museums to replace reality and manufacture myths about the colonisers and the colonised that justified and reified colonialism. Colonialism through the appropriation of objects and narratives about the colonised was presented as a natural or anthropological outcome of history, through the disciplines of ethnography and science. Thus, he suggests that museums of nonnatural history are needed that are the result of sympathy for rather than power over the colonised. Museums that might be curated around redress and reparation of the irreparable. Cave_bureau suggests a parallel imagined institution, the Benevolent Reparations Institute (BRIT), that will provide a new Imagination Fund for Africa, which will attract the return of stolen wealth to Global South for the use of arts and funding of the *Maasai Cow Corridor*. The fund will not rely on Western guilt but will draw back extracted wealth through a reversed pull of what they call 'remedial acts of reverse futurism.' Critical to this architectural practice is the return of imagination and the foregrounding of resistant acts to counter colonial geotrauma. The geologic is included as a partner in the healing.

Alongside the reverse futurism of The Anthropocene Museums that would need to be first imagined and then built to attest to the histories of colonial geotraumas, Cave_bureau's practice gives us a cartography of possibility: routes that de-border marginalising geographies and de-couple the segregations between human and non-human life. Cave_bureau engages with the cave as a space of resistance as well as trauma, calling on the site as not only defined by the East African trade in enslaved persons but equally conversant with the architecture of the Mau Mau fighters and their forest retreat outside the oppressive state.

Thinking with epistemologies of revolutionary forest geology and the Earth practices of the marginalised is not simply about acknowledging often buried histories but part of recognising how the oppressed have always been more attentive to the actual context of the Earth because that attention was the way to materially build paths to freedom. Familiarity with environmental epistemologies and ecological knowledges of the forest and caves are part of an organisation of political insurgency and the survival of anticolonial forces. Channelling the affective resonance of that anticoloniality as a located architecture is one way to insist on the specificity of space against its rationalisation in colonial or neocolonial logics of abstraction. This is the critical force of what a museum should be, Cave_bureau insists. The Shimoni Caves, "where walls tell a sad tale" (as it reads on the visitors sign) of the Eastern trade in enslaved persons, is also part of a bigger underground architecture in the larger complexes of the rift valley, and thus in the larger spatialities of its possibilities and histories. The resonances of spatial complexity can be mobilised to generate new futures that are not solely contained nor constrained by violent pasts.

Racial capitalism

Architecture and its geological impacts are a part of material practices of dehumanisation and subjugation. Not just in the mines or in the processes of extraction and clearance, but also in the psychic work of exclusion and displacement. Architecture is part of flattening of imaginative capacities and attachments of Indigenous peoples through constriction and carceral geographies, like the designation of national parks with their colonial conservation models of displacement, replacement and re-interpretation of nature as spectacle. This is demonstrated in Nairobi and Maasai Mara National Park, Kenya, where people and planet perform in a colonial dream of charismatic megafauna in the 'beginnings of nature.' They imagined petrified worlds of pristine nature, the conceit and titillation of 'forgotten' worlds, land of the lost style. Big cat landscape as animal trophy scene, nature as cinema.

The *Maasai Cow Corridor* organises around the movement that was arrested and petrified in the carceral spatialities of national parks (and that which continues in the white African 'safari' tradition). Where the 'original' peoples of the Maasai are presented as part of the spectacle of nature imagined as arrested in time for colonial contemplation, the cow corridor restores the right to movement to the urban inhabitants, removing the privilege of cars and capital to circulate the city. Nairobi was used as a source for water for cattle before the construction of the colonial railway established it in 1899 as a colonial administrative centre. Debordering colonial containment by British colonial authorities in 'reserves' for 'selected' Indigenous peoples (the Maasai) who were displaced (and continue to be displaced) from their ancestral lands is a move towards unsettling the legacy effect of colonial architectures in their neocolonial guises. The original inhabitants of the city are restored along new cave routes, to traverse, visit vets and salt licks and follow their grazing paths and water routes.

There is significant divergence and diasporas of colonial architectures in its historic and present formations. It is nonetheless resurgent and thus the site of continued forms of control and ongoing divestment of marginalised peoples and practices. Nairobi as a city emerged out of a colonial plan built around an imagined railway with Uganda to connect then British colonial territories and bring geomaterials out.

The colonial segregation 1948 Masterplan[5] organised urban

planning around the division between the races, between European private estates and unrestricted areas for Asians and Africans, with government quarries and the establishment of 'reserves.' The plan spatially prioritised suburbs, whereby Kenyan tribes were displaced to make way for leisure activities and golf. Temporary employment contracts in the city of Nairobi, discouraged settlement in the city and led to the rise of informal settlements with little infrastructure. Built onto structural-spatial inequalities that were stratified and consolidated by colonial planning, legacies of racial zoning and unsettlement of workers connect across Africa to American urban cities. Colonial removals have ongoing echoes when Western dominated urbanism becomes the aspirational model of city development with its selective forms of reconstruction under the apartheids of capital, with little attention to the ongoing dispossession of the poor or reparative ecological futures.

Racial capitalism is that colonial mode of enacting extraction through racialised zones, internal and external, to maintain a particular form of existence. Racial capitalism needs architectural forms to be materially manifested as an aspiration and a dream of futurity. The maintenance of racial hierarchies is made at the expense of subjects designated outside its spatialising zones of active and influential political subjectivity. It is a form of social subjugation constructed as a restrictive spatial dynamic that is auxiliary to a centralisation of power that is mobilised as spatial influence, communication, persuasion and as a site of mobility that marginalises other forms of movement.

An architectural practice of freedom
In 2021, the new Railway City plan to expand the central business district with the construction of a 425-acre urban development was designed by UK architects as part of a public-private partnership deal with UK Export Finance and the Railway City Development Authority, Kenya Railways Corporation and the Nairobi Metropolitan Services. According to the UK Foreign Secretary James Cleverly (born 1969), who spoke during the groundbreaking of the site, Nairobi Railway City will serve as a template for other projects that

the UK seeks to implement in Africa. 'Africa rising' is imagined as an economic telos and opportunity, amid models of population growth, such as in the journal *The Lancet* that predict demography models of the youngest continent (another 'Out of Africa' re-birth) and African cities with exponential population growth. The *Financial Times* defines Africa rising as a "narrative that improved governance means the continent is almost predestined to enjoy a long period of mid-to-high single-digit economic growth, rising incomes and an emerging middle class."[6]

Africa rising is the promise of middle-class economic power, associated with the democratisation of African states, made through the mobilisation of geopower out of Africa. OECD market reports on the economic power of African cities, predict that one third of Africa's per capita growth will be due to urbanism. Africa's cities have tripled in size since 1990 and "urbanisation is an opportunity for Africa", "realising the economic potential of African cities"[7] through neoliberal urban development and neocolonial debt financing. Such an imagination for the city participates and perpetuates in the unequal distribution of environmental effects and the affective exclusion that the city mobilises through its prioritising of capital accumulative infrastructures.

Not only does decolonising architecture require the instantiation of its negative spaces of construction and its forms of communication, but also it requires the destabilisation of the object-form of architecture and its claims to a bounded space. That is, architecture has rearranged the planet's over- and underground through a particular colonial axis of extraction, so the story of urbanism is not just one of sprawl and densities, but the verticalities and depth of urban material mobilisation. Some of these verticalities are actual/physical, as with the mineshaft, and some are figurative/metaphorical/literal about depths of subjugation that oppressive spatial dynamics entail, from lack of basic water and sanitation to the physical and mental misery of poverty and constricted forms of life.

The practice of Cave_bureau offers a serious and sincere architecture for addressing geotrauma and its erasures in the urban fabric of the African city, a manifesto for worlding inside the progeny of geologic time for a more possible Earth.

While the focus of decolonial acts has often been on the restitution of symbolic loot rather than attention to the dynamics of financial and material extraction, the acknowledgement of geotrauma requires an engagement with not just what is taken but what is left behind, and that which grows around extraction and erasure. The relations, practices and materialities that grow in and around the seismic wake of geotrauma is how extraction as a colonial practice continues to live in the present. Cave_bureau offers an affective architecture that acknowledges and builds with this geotrauma, to offer restorative pathways to healing the scars of geographic and geological trauma, materialising architectures of futurity that strengthen resident claims to existence before and beyond colonialism and its neocolonial kin. Prototyping ancestral urbanisms, their cow corridor explicitly engages Maasai-cow practices in the present of their ongoing marginalisation, bringing the underground overground, enacting a series of movements through and in the city. It is an architectural practice of freedom in the geotrauma of colonial afterlives and for the future of their repair.

Notes

1   Sylvia Wynter et al., "Unparalleled Catastrophe for Our Species? Or, to Give Humanness a Different Future: Conversations," *Sylvia Wynter: On Being Human as Praxis* (Duke University Press: Durham, 2015), 68.
2   Sylvia Wynter et al., 25.
3   Cave_bureau, Homepage, accessed December 2022, https://www.cave.co.ke.
4   Kathryn Yusoff, *Geologic Life: Inhuman Intimacy and the Geophysics of Race* (Duke University Press, Forthcoming).
5   L. W. Thornton White, L. Silberman and P. R. Anderson, *Nairobi: The Masterplan, A Report prepared for the Municipal Council of Nairobi,* (London: H.M. Stationery Office, 1948).
6   Steve Johnson, "Slowdown calls 'Africa rising' narrative into question," *Financial Times*, 27 October 2015.
7   *Africa's Urbanisation Dynamics 2022,* (OECD/ United Nations, 2022), 15, https://www.oecd. org/publications/africa- surbanisation-dynamics- 2022-3834ed5b-en.htm.

Kathryn Yusoff is professor of inhuman geography in the school of geography at Queen Mary, University of London, UK. Her research examines how inhuman and nonorganic materialities have consequences for how we understand issues of environmental change, race and subjectivity. She is author of several books and articles, among these *A Billion Black Anthropocenes or None* (University of Minnesota Press, 2018) and the forthcoming *Geologic Life: Inhuman Intimacies and the Geophysics of Race* (Duke University Press), which addresses the racial geologies of rocks. She is recipient of the Association of American Geographers 2022 Award for Creativity in Geography.

08

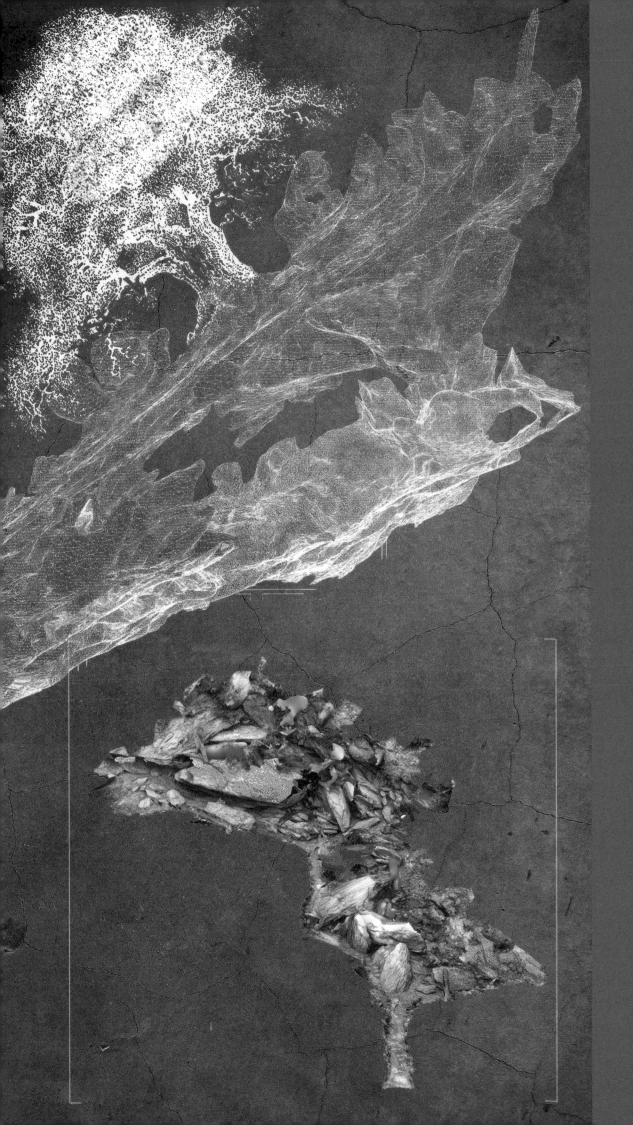

Reinscribing
New York City

The Anthropocene Museum 5.0

For this instalment we intersect an ongoing academic standpoint to expand on the current discourse to re-asses, re-dress and re-imagine museum mapping and making in the putrid and wretched age of the Anthropocene. With a cohort of eleven students from Columbia University's Graduate School of Architecture Planning and Preservation, we set out on a cave surveying exercise of two Native American caves of the Lenape people on Manhattan Island: Ramble Cave in Central Park, and the Inwood Hill Park Caves.

Our syllabus looked to confront the histories of Indigenous cultural extractions intertwined with the history of museology, within the seemingly innocuous curation of artwork and artefacts, which operated on a global scale during imperial and colonial times decimating many lives, cultures and environments. We invited students to reflect on the disruptive operations of restitution of stolen artefacts, as a disjointed practice of what we call 'reverse curation'. A practice to inclusively coordinate the return of stolen artefacts that factor in the nuances of human trauma, resistance and healing on multiple socio-geological and architectural scales, necessary to shape what a museum and, by extension, the re-reading of 'civilisation' in this epoch could, and probably should, be.

Using new grammars of geology, students used multiscaled terraforming and archaeological tools to recalibrate the museum through interventions at the modular and intimate scale, to the broader urban and ecological scale. Students took a critical look at European imperial and colonial legacies of erasure when looking at the birth of the city through what geologist Kathryn Yusoff aptly calls 'earth writing'.

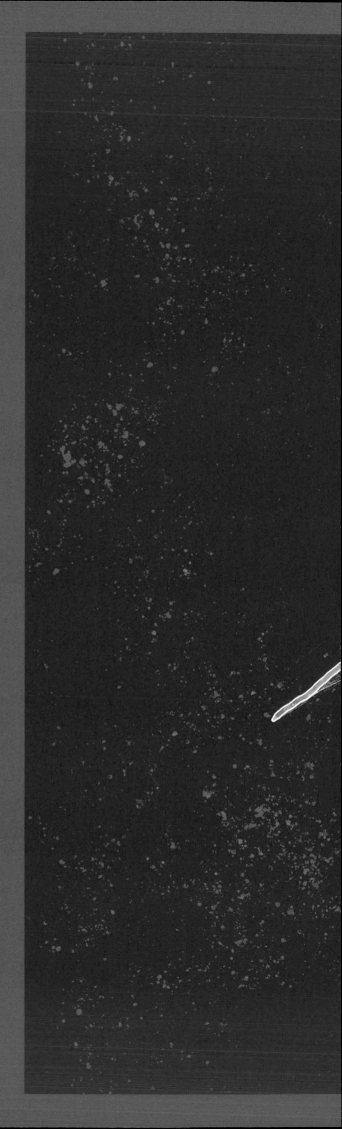

Anthropocene Museum 5.0: *Reinscribing New York City*, New York City, US, 2022. Koozarch interview and student work showcase.

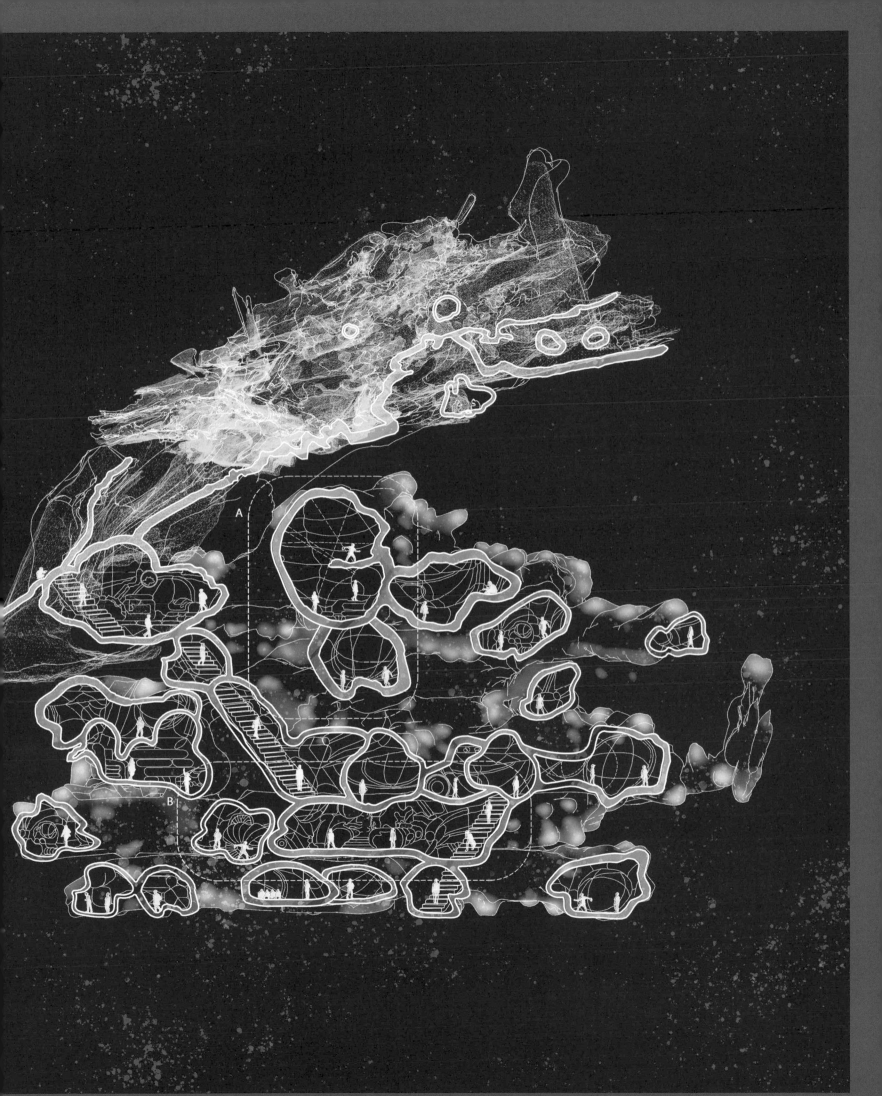

From the cave surveying exercise with students from Columbia University's Graduate School of
Architecture Planning and Preservation (G3APP).
A: © Claire Koh; B: © Niriksha Shetty; C: © Sixue Long.

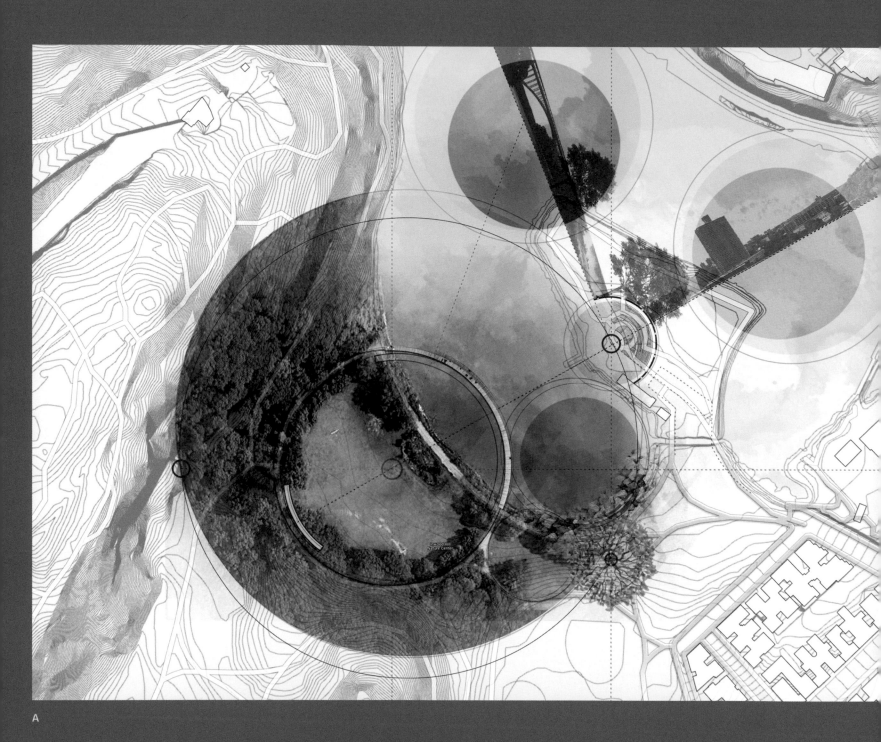

A

B

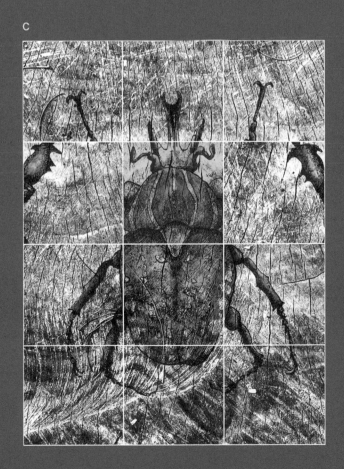

C

D

E

F

TOPOLOGY PATTERN - SPACIALIZATION

IN DESIGNING THE LOWER SPACE OF THE CAVE, THE UNIQUE TOPOGRAPHIC PATTERN OF THE INWOOD CAVE WAS USED. AN ATYPICAL SPACE WAS DESIGNED SO THAT THE LOWER SPACE COULD BE ORGANICALLY WOVEN WITH TREES, STONES, AND TOPOGRAPHY.

THE CENTRAL SPACE IS A RESIDENCE WHERE PEOPLE ARE PROVIDED WITH COMFORT THROUGH TUBES. AT THE BOTTOM, WATER GATHERS USING THE SLOPE OF THE CAVE. THE GATHERING PLACE BECOMES A WATER HOLDING CHAMBER AND SUPPLIES WATER TO THE SURROUNDING SPACE.

THROUGH THE ROLE OF SUPPLYING WATER AND THE CONNECTION OF DISTANT SPACES, THE INTERIOR CAN BE FORMED MORE SYSTEMATICALLY.

TERRAIN

NATURAL TREE ROOTS

TOPOGRAPHY

COMFORT SYSTEM

STREAM COLLECTOR

MAIN WATER CHAMBER

DOWN STREAM COLLECTOR

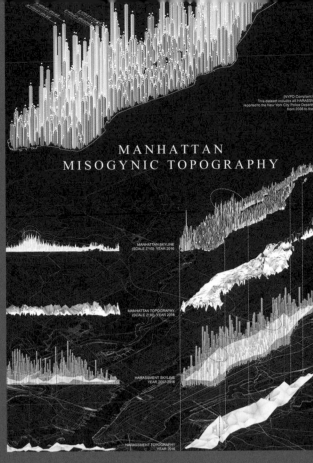

MANHATTAN
MISOGYNIC TOPOGRAPHY

Temporary Exhibitions

What would happen if the human scale was no longer the protagonist of the space? I documented my own exploration process in ramble cave, a process of placing myself on the site, on the basis of which a new set of modular illustrations can be developed, challenging the existing modular logic, where rocks, trees, and rivers can become the protagonists.

J

K

L

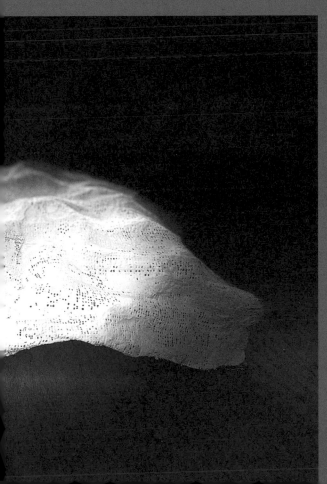

Freedom
Forest

The Anthropocene Museum 6.0

In parallel to Salone del Mobile, Milan's Furniture Fair, Prada Frames hosted a symposium in 2022 that delved into the complex relationship between the natural environment and design. The programme was curated by Formafantasma, a research and design studio based in Milan and Rotterdam. Prada Frames brought together the valuable contribution of scholars and professionals, such as scientists, architects, designers, artists, activists, anthropologists and law experts.

The symposium took place at the Biblioteca Nazionale Braidense in Milan, which holds one of the largest and most important, forest-fed book collections in the world, though against the backdrop of a furniture fair that is largely fed by the global timber industry's environmentally destructive legacy. The short film *Freedom Forest* presented the colonial complexity to this backdrop, celebrating the Kenyan ancestral relationship to forests that was always sustainable and where oral histories were narrated in song and word around fires, not enshrined in books.

We walked through the enigmatic Ololua Forest on the outskirts of Nairobi in a place called Karen, situated adjacent to what were the occupied settler plantations, owned by the Danish author Karen Blixen (1885-1962). This forest were sites of refuge for the Mau Mau freedom fighters during the struggle for independence. Karen Blixen left Kenya in 1931, with three different families later owning the farm. In 1963, when Kenya became independent, the Danish state bought the farm and donated it to the National Museum of Kenya. In 1986 the farm was made into a museum.

We interviewed Muthoni Likimani (born 1926), one of the freedom fighting mothers, among other matriarchs all compiled as an oral record of our history that is seldom narrated for future generations to understand, and for the Prada Frames, as a counter archive that was narrated in the library, albeit for a brief moment in time.

Anthropocene Museum 6.0: *Freedom Forest*, Ololua Forest, Kenya, 2022. Exhibition, Biblioteca Nazionale Braidense, Milan, for Prada & Formafantasma, short film.

Pages 122-123: The Freedom Fighter, Field Marshal Muthoni wa Kirima (born 1931), after emerging from the forest in 1963 to lay down arms at the flag of free Kenya at Ruringu Stadium, Nyeri, Kenya.
Cave_bureau mapped the protected natural reserve lands of forests and grasslands in Kenya coloured in bright green, while in red is the route taken by the British 'Lunatic Express' railway line, built between 1896-1901. The sole purpose of the railway was to move westwards along Kenya's Indian Ocean coastline, to secure the source of the River Nile, the so-called Lake Victoria, originally named Nam Lolwe by the native Luo community. Along the way resistance to these anthropogenic pressures, came in the form of the man-eating lions of Tsavo, malaria-carrying mosquitos and the local Indigenous population.
Stella Mutegi and Kabage Karanja visit the forests of Ololua to reflect on their ancestral relationship to the land.

Cave_bureau, stills from Anthropocene Museum 2.0: *Shimoni Slave Caves* short film. Source of the Nile, Lake Victoria in Kenya. Early settler explorations and an early Luo community canoe.
Post-independency, *Daily Nation* newspaper cover, Kenya.
For the short film *Freedom Fighters*, Cave_bureau interviewed the Mau Mau freedom fighter, Muthoni Likimani (born 1926), who fought against British colonialism.

Culture Postponed? Postcolonial Arts and Culture Institution Building in Kenya

By Joy Mboya

At independence, there was a nation that was a geographic and a political entity, without a specific cultural identity.
– Gichora Mwangi, theatre scholar and practitioner[1]

As arts and culture from Kenya and Africa become more visible in the global arena, interest also arises about the institutions, structures and spaces on the African continent that incubate, disseminate and promote African artists and their arts. While there may be common experiences of cultural institution formation across the continent, each geography, each nation is unique.

The way in which culture has been handled in the postcolonial state is significant in the formation of arts and culture spaces in Kenya. The unfoldment of contemporary arts and culture institutions occurs within a movement of ethnic communities coming into collective political, economic, social and cultural being during the colonial period and after. The trajectory of arts institutions and cultural infrastructure is entangled in Kenya's independence and national development discourse. Therefore, a richer and more comprehensive discussion on the state and evolution of Kenyan contemporary arts and culture organisations is better made when contextualised within a postcolonial period, but also when it is read critically against the present-day social reality that arts organisations and spaces operate in. Situating arts and culture institutions in this manner often means that to engage art is to also comment on, and even sometimes directly influence, enfolded issues that overlay and intersect with arts and culture in important ways.

Most of Africa's modern states are barely fifty years old, the same period marking independence from European colonialism and covering two generations of 'independent Africans.' The cohesion of the new states has been tested by political conflicts, ethnic animosities, natural disasters, neocolonialism, globalisation and population growth. African cultures, and their arts within it, as the repository of identities, values and knowledge have not been a priority in this flux until lately, when the concept of an African creative economy has begun to enter the policy and development agendas of African governments.

Culture and nation building in the postcolonial state

Through the 1950s and into the 1960s, as African states struggled for political independence, the continent's freedom movements invoked culture as an essential starting point for shaping ideology for Africa's new states. The philosophies and thinking of Black writers such as Frantz Fanon (1925-1961), Aimé Césaire (1913-2008), Léopold Sédar Senghor (1906-2001) and others, inspired and informed the anchoring of culture in African freedom movements. Culture was perceived to be a solid foothold for building national consciousness and maintaining African values.

Thus, on gaining independence, various permutations of African political ideology, derived from African values, took shape. Such ideologies were meant to nurture new national identities and collective values in erstwhile colonial territories. However, a cultural transformation and consolidation of national magnitude would require focussed intentionality, something many new African states struggled with. Kenya adopted a philosophy of African socialism, published by the Kenyan government in 1965, defined as a system that draws "on the best of African traditions" yet is "adaptable to new and rapidly changing circumstances."[2] But this guiding document made no mention of culture, and did not articulate any unifying cultural vision to envelop over forty diverse ethnic communities existing under the umbrella of the Kenyan nation. At most, the document referred to the establishment of tourism policies and national agencies to encourage visitors to Kenya's natural heritage of beaches and mountains.

Under African socialism, the new state now prioritised political and economic imperatives. While recognising the inevitability of continuing relationships and exchange with countries and cultures that were former colonial powers, Kenya's African socialism emphasised that development in Kenya should not be a satellite dependency with an external country or group of countries. Additionally, the document stated that co-option of technological knowledge and proven methods from elsewhere should be "without commitment, without strings and without political domination"[3] to uphold Kenya's political and economic independence.

The true outcome of events is, of course, evident in the state of Kenya's politics and economy today. Colonialism was dismantled only in a superficial way and Kenya fell straight into the tight grip of neocolonialism, which alongside other consequential internal forces and circumstances have defined the nation's trajectory.

When Kenya gained independence in 1963 it inherited key cultural institutions from the colonial state: the National Museums of Natural History and Ethnography, the Kenya Conservatoire of Music and the Kenya National Theatre, among others. Interestingly, by the time independence was achieved, there was not yet a national arts gallery or national arts museum in the colony. But there were other cultural infrastructures such as cinemas, libraries, social halls and private playhouses that carried over into the postcolonial state as well. These institutions, symbols and conduits of a western cultural episteme and soft power, became the default foundational institutions of culture at public-sector level as the new Kenya state offered no ready-made counter cultural ideology.

Even the vigorous Africanisation policy that Kenya carried out soon after independence, to propel Africans into public service positions and jobs, and ownership of businesses and land, was not applied to culture. With culture 'postponed' no new investments were made in arts and cultural institutions for nearly fifty years. Instead, culture in Kenya became a place of tension and contention, especially in ethnicised politics, while the arts – if not ignored or taken for granted – were viewed as seditious activity against the state. Government censorship in the 1980s and 1990s silenced cultural voices or forced their exile and banned political dissent.

Yet, while at the level of the state culture appeared shelved, everyday cultural life and traditions of Kenya's communities continued, though changing and adapting on account of a period of colonial domination followed by postcolonial modernity. These living cultural expressions were institutionalised, structured and formalised within their communities, giving distinctiveness and a sense of belonging to community members. Such institutionalised cultural realities were mostly intangible and not visible in brick-and-mortar vehicles such as a museum, or an arts institution. But they had nevertheless a constitutive

and performative power to centre identities, define cultural taste and influence cultural production.

Without investments in arts and culture – typically achieved by the public sector through an arts education strategy, the provision of cultural infrastructure and cultural institution-building – a phase of relative stasis ensued, hindering the flourishing of arts in Kenya.

So local creative expressions, lacking an overarching cultural vision and guiding policy, became de-contextualised by taking the "form of museum or tourist-oriented culture".[4] Such de-contextualised expressions were experienced in carry-over institutionalised events such as the annual educational drama and music festivals (which had their genesis in the Kenya colony) or museum-like spaces such as the Bomas of Kenya, which is a village that was established by the Kenya government in the 1970s as a tourist centre where the cultures of Kenya are put on display through music and dance performances and reproduction of life in traditional homesteads. Under such circumstances, according to Gichora Mwangi, the Kenyan theatre scholar, a false fossilised tradition was presented because of the state not providing a cultural development framework for a socio-political and cultural milieu in flux. More recently, of course, spaces such as the Bomas of Kenya and the Kenya National Theatre are changing through novel, contemporary programming by African directors and curators.

Culture advanced? Towards confident cultural inhabitations

The conundrum for artists and arts institutions was how to define a new cultural reality for themselves. One approach in forging new directions was to experiment and innovate local creative expressions. The university was a key site for this exploration. For instance, university-based free travelling theatres of Kenya and Uganda in the 1980s moved theatre away from the institutional structure of the National Theatre and took performances into villages. This was a different way of making theatre and engaging audiences by innovating an endogenous community orature practice which utilises song, dance and narration to drive the performance.

With the introduction of multi-party politics in 2002, a wind of change was blowing. Kenya's bilateral partners, and international foundations in the arts and culture field took an interest in the sector in

Kenya, initially as an avenue to expand the awareness and agency of ordinary citizens in matters of democracy and human rights. With funding now available for cultural exchanges and training, cultural production and audience development from these sources, something new entered the picture – the possibility to create organisations and institutions in the arts to undertake these aims. Also stronger by this time was advocacy from artists, culture practitioners and arts organisations for a policy and legislative environment conducive to the flowering of artistic expression and a contemporary culture.

Through the entry of donor-partners into the scene, several new arts and culture spaces, organisations and institutions came into being. A number of these, while possessing a core vision to promote and advance the arts in one or another way, included advocacy in their practice. They were consistent in taking action to ensure that cultural policy environment was enabling.

Owing to the lack – for too long – of associated formative education and training in arts and culture, another characteristic acquired by some of these arts organisations was to serve as sites of artistic training and experimentation. As such, some have even provided complementary infrastructure in the form of production and rehearsal spaces. Naturally the dissemination of cultural works – exhibitions, performances and so on – is yet another role that these organisations undertake.

In other words, a cadre of arts and culture institutions and organisations that are hybrid in practice have evolved. They are engaging in policy discourses; offering training through workshops and residencies; and providing spaces for creative concept development, rehearsal and production; and they are responsive to present day socio-cultural exigencies.

Sustained advocacy has also yielded positive outcomes. A cultural policy has been formulated and copyright laws to protect artistic expression have been legislated. They point to a growing recognition and integration of arts and culture by government in its policy planning. However, an elephant remains in the room: the sustainability of Kenya's arts and culture organisations. Despite an improving policy environment, public sector financial support for the arts is still not forthcoming, and donor-partners are not a long-term solution to the viability of Kenyan arts and culture spaces and institutions. Their survival and longevity are existential questions.

In *Panya Routes* (2022), the South Africa-based scholar and artist Kim Gurney's research into the current practices of selected arts institutions across the continent offers an insightful perspective on their organisational structure, operating principles and survival:

[Independent arts spaces in Africa] operate collaboratively, with a regional emphasis and with a non-profit basis that is formalized in a co-operative structure to work towards common and more equitable social ends. Either way artists are the main constituents, and arts practice and process drive the organizational thinking. [...] Public sector support in these contexts is negligible or non-existent.[5]

Looking at five formalised independent arts spaces in Tanzania, Ethiopia, Ghana and Egypt together with the GoDown Arts Centre in Nairobi, Kenya (of which the undersigned is the director), Gurney finds that "through a combination of strategic refusals and creative reimaginations [these spaces] reach for social imaginaries in excess of the status quo."[6] The arts spaces go beyond what already exists to "instantiate new contexts and possibilities and disrupt conventional notions of sustainability [...] to better inhabit a future that has already arrived."[7] This they do by deploying what she has extracted as five 'working principles' in her study: 'Horizontality' describes how these art spaces exhibit organisational approaches that invite multiple views in a non-hierarchical way, and value local ingenuity. 'Reuse or second chance' refers to how the arts organisations inhabit/adapt physical spaces for arts and culture purposes, but it also refers to reuse of materials in art making. 'Performativity' examines the power of the practice of these organisations to activate situations and people. 'Elasticity,' speaks to the flexibility, adaptiveness and responsiveness of the arts spaces to changing circumstances. And the fifth principle, 'convergence', is about the ability of these spaces to consolidate their practice between the past and the present.

Gurney's astute observation and analysis brings a fresh angle to the discourse on arts practice in Africa today. Though the study identifies shared working principles among the arts spaces, there is clear understanding too that these principles will vary in degree of manifestation as they will be coloured by the specific vision, history and context of each space.

The GoDown Arts Centre: perspectives from within

The GoDown Arts Centre, a Kenyan arts institution that has existed for two decades, encapsulates these 'working principles' in its practice, and illustrates the evolution of an arts space in the latter part of Kenya's half century of independence. At the Centre we prioritise arts programming, provision of infrastructure and space, education, advocacy and contributing to social change through the intersection of community and culture. The GoDown operates across scale, physically and temporally, and across artistic and social values. Its programmes exist within the physical centre, and equally beyond in externally programmed community spaces and collaborating sites. Taking action and learning iteratively, it has come to position its work and purpose within the idea that communities do progress when they nurture their arts and culture and that their individual community members, who, as units of community are cultural producers and cultural innovators, should be accorded space and freedom to be so confidently.

This placement (that manifests Gurney's principle of 'horizontality') underscores the GoDown's conviction of the vital importance that Kenyan peoples be enabled to build their cultural confidence and view their own cultural inhabitations as valid and generative of salient ideas and knowledge. Cultural confidence is a factor of sustainability for the GoDown as the future of the institution will rest to a significant extent on local support and local investments in its programmes and activities.

The matter of institution building is a continuing area of learning for the GoDown. The GoDown's current legal form – nonprofit, public purpose – belies the explorative way in which its practice has evolved. In the process of coming into being, the institution has made several realisations that have contributed to shaping its ethos and its vision.

Its relationship with artists and the arts organisations who work from within its compound represents 'a community of practice' but equally they are autonomous and at liberty to advance their aims independently. It is a self-contained physical space, yet it is nested within a layered

Joy Mboya is a Kenyan cultural actor and architect. She is co-founder and executive director of the GoDown Arts Centre in Nairobi, Kenya. She has led the centre's development as a site for artistic experimentation, cross-sector partnerships and creative collaboration since 2003.

'meta space'[8] comprising the wider community, city and nation with which it has fundamental bonds.

As arts organisations and spaces proliferate in Kenya and in Africa, different models will no doubt emerge. Digital technologies and the internet are permeating and changing practically all aspects of human endeavour, including the arts. In the burgeoning population of African youth, whose access to digital technology expands year by year, and who are recasting their cultural identities and resources in speculative future worlds, virtual and real, lie potentialities of an exciting cultural reality we can only guess at.

Yet this future striving will need to contend with the current digital dominance of Western big tech companies on the African continent. Kenyan arts spaces are already visualising their form and their role in the new digital frontiers, and most especially trying to understand and secure the battlefronts of data ethics and data protection. A statement made in Kenya's African socialism planning document in 1965 is still relevant and applicable to these spaces today: "[Our] ultimate objectives are never fully attained. Every time one target is attained a new one becomes necessary. Indeed, we forever live in transition."[9]

Notes

1   Gichora Mwangi, *Orature in Contemporary Theatre Practice in Kenya* (University of Leeds, 1996), 110.

2   Republic of Kenya, *African Socialism and its Application to Planning in Kenya*, Sessional Paper No. 10 of 1965, Government Printers, 1965, https://repository.kippra.or.ke/handle/123456789/2345.

3   Republic of Kenya, *African Socialism*

4   Mwangi, 138.

5   Kim Gurney, *Panya Routes* (Motto Books, 2022), 14.

6   Gurney, 16.

7   Gurney, 16.

8   Mwangi.

9   Republic of Kenya, *African Socialism.*

New Age
Africana

The Anthropocene Museum 7.0

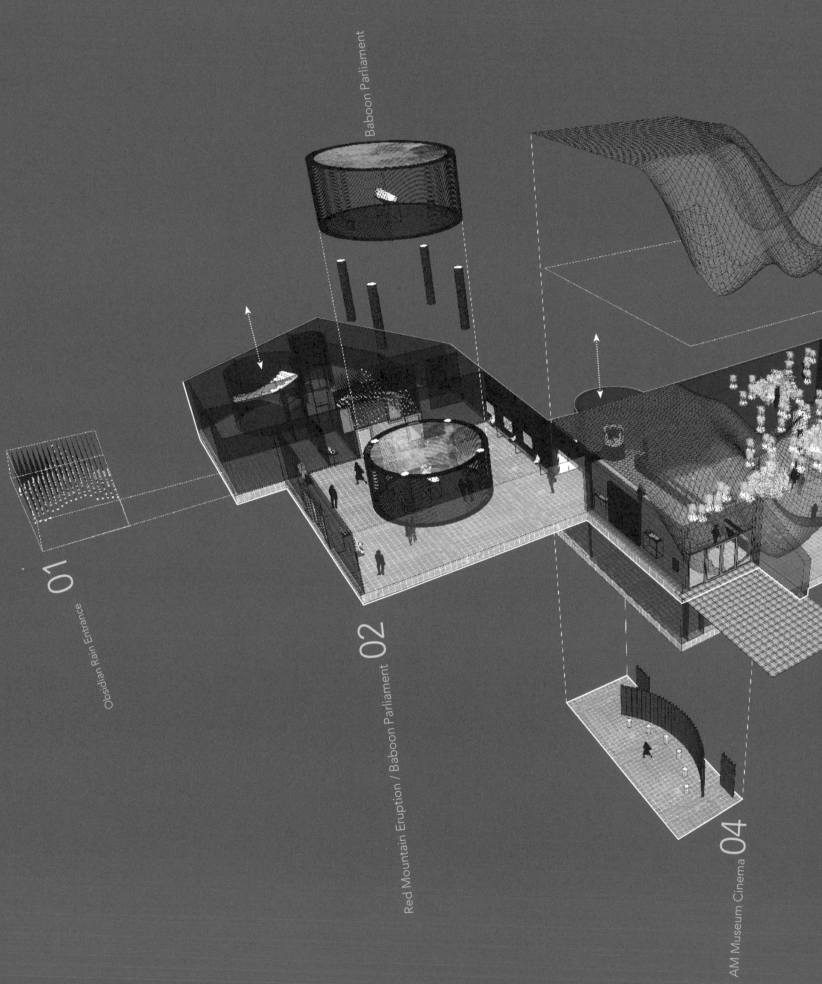

01

Obsidian Rain Entrance

Baboon Parliament

02

Red Mountain Eruption / Baboon Parliament

04

AM Museum Cinema

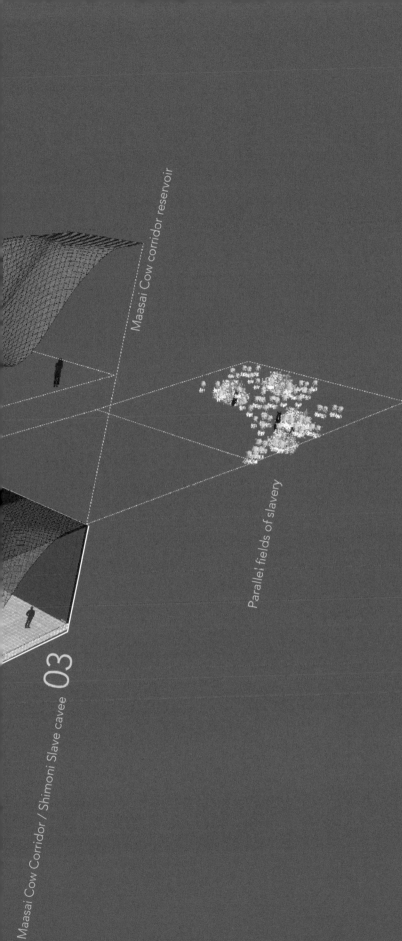

Maasai Cow corridor reservoir

Parallel fields of slavery

Maasai Cow Corridor / Shimoni Slave cavee 03

We describe *The Architect's Studio* exhibition at Louisiana Museum of Modern Art as a collective effort of exhibition planning and experiments in museology. At its heart is the collaboration between two museum institutions, which is fundamentally a microcosm of repair between the divided progeny of our shared human ancestors who left Africa, and those who remained on the continent. A joint effort to confront the complicated times of imperial and colonial transgression that Denmark shared, while revisiting the times of trauma that cross-sectioned multiple lands, cultures and so-called past civilisations. It is an exploration into the potential of architecture to generate pathways to read trauma and healing; an invitation to the audience to look at new ways to read a museum beyond the confines of any building to bring us together.

Several readings of the caves has led to collaborative installations, which through materials and techniques from both Kenya and Denmark has opened conjoined histories of the West and East African slave trades. The Anthropocene Museum 7.0 is an introduction and opening of a new age museum typology and programme that began on the continent of Africa almost eight years ago, and ancestrally even further back, migrating outside the continent and now returning to manifest in the last instalment of Anthropocene Museum 10.0 in the Great Rift Valley.

Anthropocene Museum 7.0: *New Age Africana*, Shimoni Slave Cave, Kenya, 2022–2023.
Exhibition at Louisiana Museum of Modern Art, short film, installations.

The Door of No Return. Ghana's Cape coast castle in West Africa, where Denmark traded slaves in the mid-eighteenth century. Cave_bureau transposed the Door of No Return to Louisiana Museum of Modern Art for closer reflection.

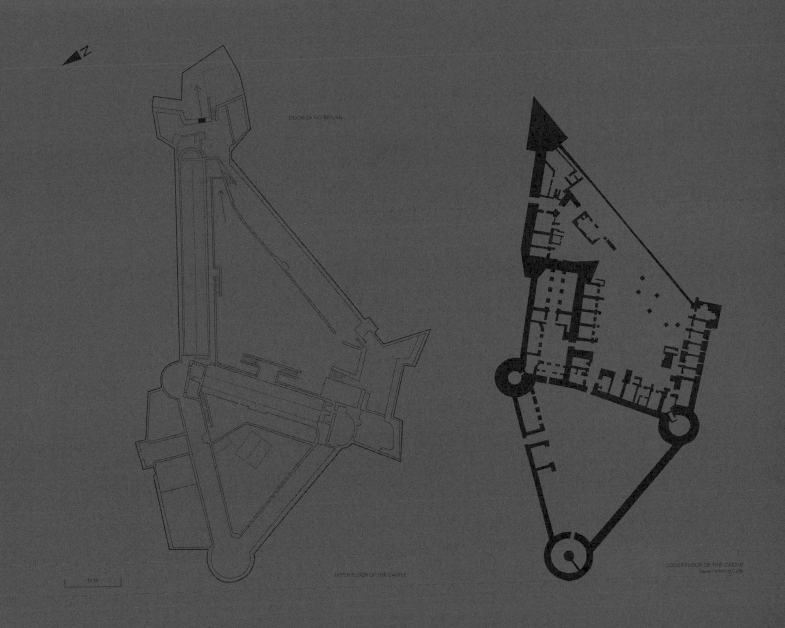

DOOR OF NO RETURN

UPPER FLOOR OF THE CASTLE

LOWER FLOOR OF THE CASTLE
Slave Holding Cells

10 M

According to Cave_bureau, architecture must be based on the knowledge of geology. Analysis of the geology around Mount Suswa, Kenya, for the installation at Louisiana Museum of Modern Art.

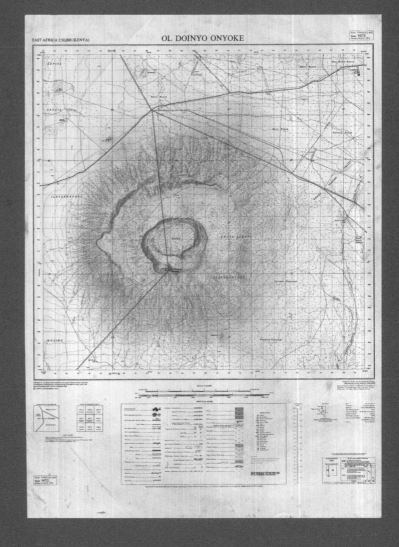

OL DOINYO ONYOKE

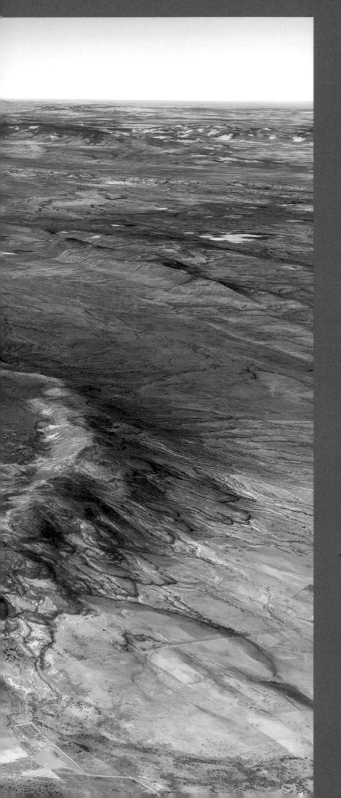

+ ECOSYSTEM
LIFE PLANT & ANIMALS

+ LOST WORLD

+ INNER CRATER
CALDERA

The artist Khadija Saye (1992-2017), tragically passed away in the Grenfell Tower fire in London, 14 June 2017. Her work *in this space we breathe*, 2017, is part of the collection of Louisiana Museum of Modern Art. Inspired by her work, Cave_bureau imagines in this project the Grenfell Tower as a growing vertical park, kept for posterity to remember the victims of fire, where birds mammals and insects can thrive as visitors walk round a new building skin.

Tower of Memory

Artefacts from the collection of Cave_bureau: Colonial Masterplan for Nairobi, 1948.
Plan for Cave_bureau, Nairobi city map's 'Origin, Void, Made.' Origin (grey), Void (yellow), Made (red),
Natural Reserve Land (green). Cave_bureau is working on the basis for their analysis of three different
types of urban spaces: Origin is the rural paradigm that most humans inhabited for millennia, but that in
recent time is left behind for the urban centres. The Void is where the majority of the origin folk live, in
the so-called slum. The Made is the former preserve of colonial settlers, where the wealthy members of
society live and work.
The painting of the decolonial activist Tom Mboya (1930-1969) by Bernard Safran (1924-1995) was
anonymously donated to The Anthropocene Museum, which was started by Cave_bureau. Transported
from the USA in transit to the exhibition at Louisiana Museum of Modern Art and then finally to Kenya.

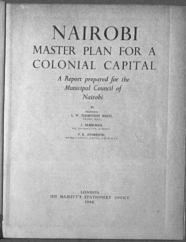

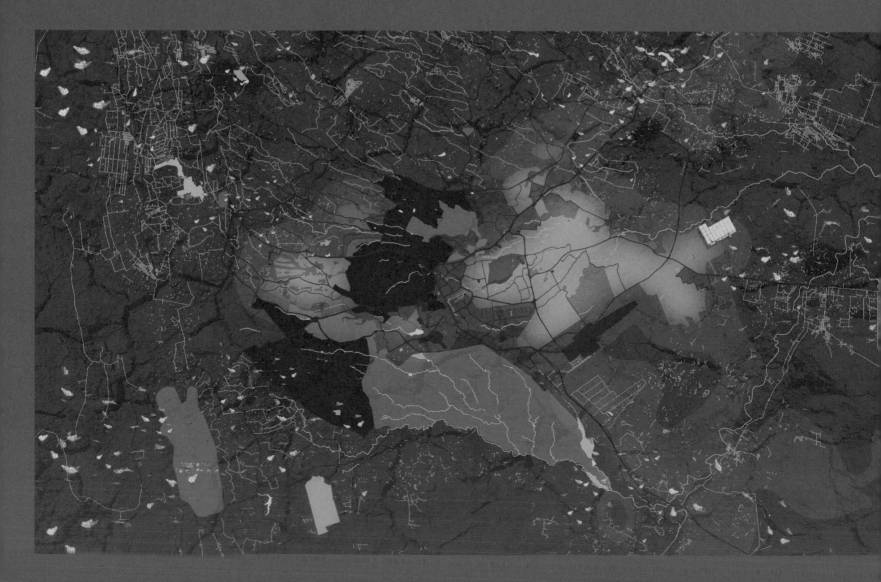

TOM MBOYA
By BERNARD SAFRAN
TIME - MARCH 7, 1960

The sketches for the Shimoni Slave Caves turned into a 1:1 weaving structure, inspired by the traditional weaving techniques of the Maasais.

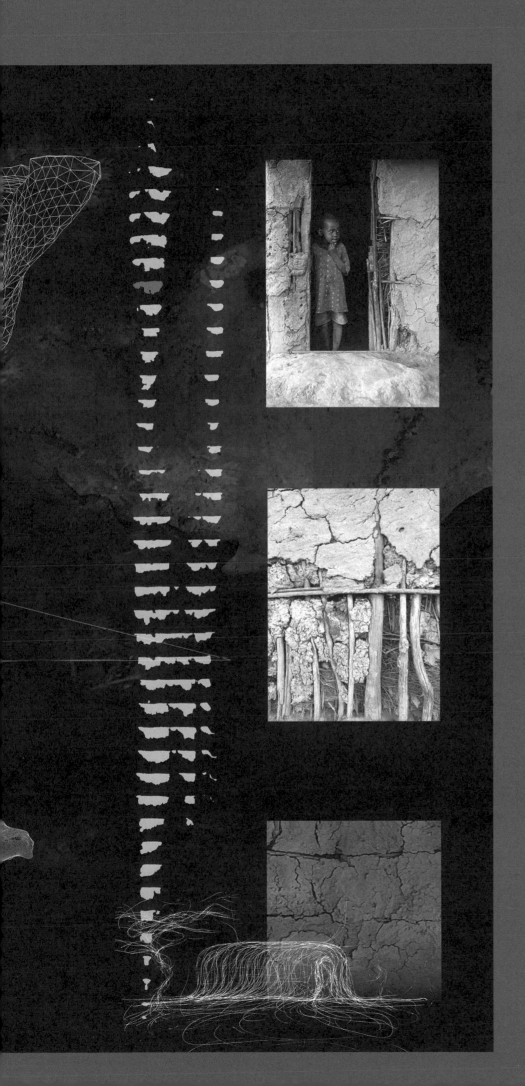

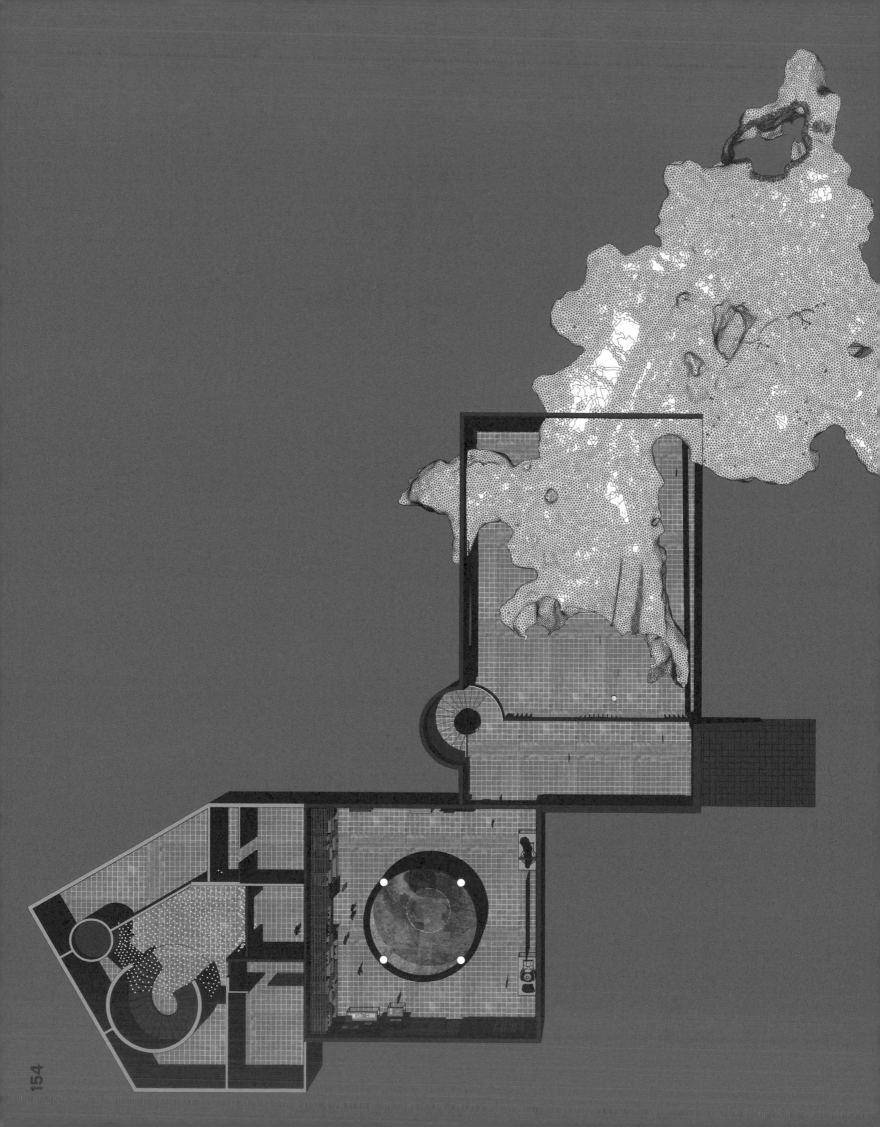

Cave_bureau, Shimoni Slave Cave scan. The Shimoni Slave Cave 3D scan bridged over the exhibition space at Louisiana Museum of Modern Art to define the section of the cave which was exhibited in 1:1. Woman performing traditional weaving technique.

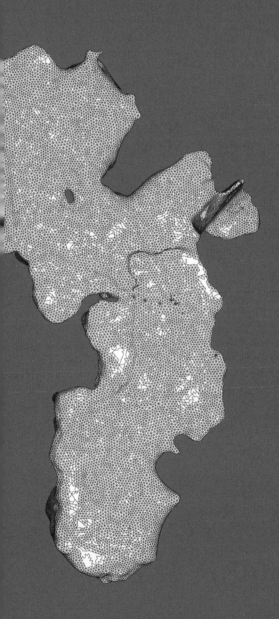

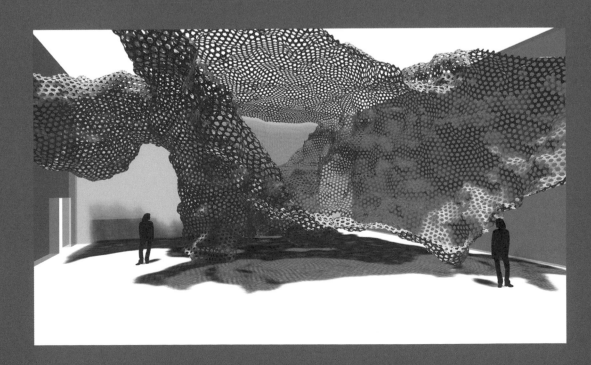

Kagome is an ancient triaxial weaving technique. The weave pattern is based on a tri-hexagonal lattice but embodies principled ways of generating double curvature through the replacement of hexagons with different polygons. Introducing lesser-sided polygons will generate elliptical curvature (like a football) and introducing greater-sided polygons will generate hyperbolic curvature (like a horse saddle). This allows complex geometries, including high genus morphologies (i.e. shapes with holes), to be approximated using straight strips of material. This is of particular interest in the context of architectural fabrication as it provides rational ways to produce complex geometry without needing to cut or form components to the target geometry.

The Chair for Biohybrid Architecture, based within the Centre for Information Technology and Architecture (CITA) at the Royal Danish Academy School of Architecture, which has been researching the translation of kagome principles into digital design tools to automate the generation of principled pattern topologies of arbitrary design targets. Within the EU funded project *Fungal Architectures*, it is explored how kagome weaves might be combined with mycelium-based (the root-like structure of a fungus) materials to develop completely novel approaches to architectural structures based on local sourcing, regenerative design and circular economy principles.

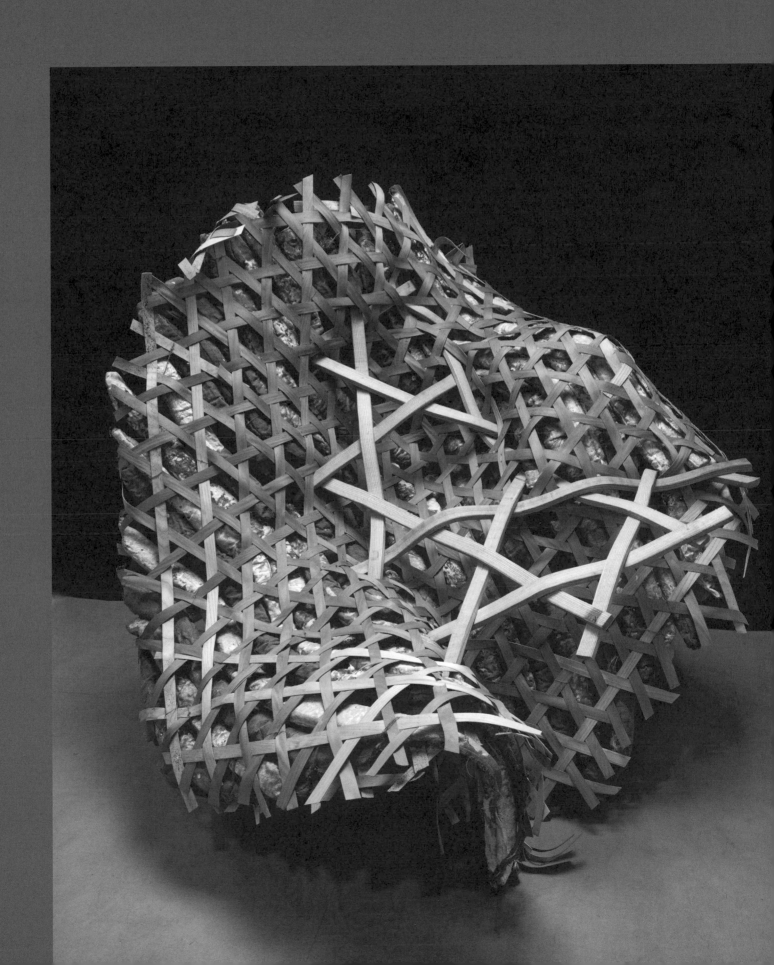

A workshop was held six months prior to the exhibition to estimate the amount of material and production time for the 300 m² hand woven installation. The 1:1 weaving was realised in collaboration with the Centre for Information Technology and Architecture (CITA) at the Royal Danish Academy, School of Architecture.

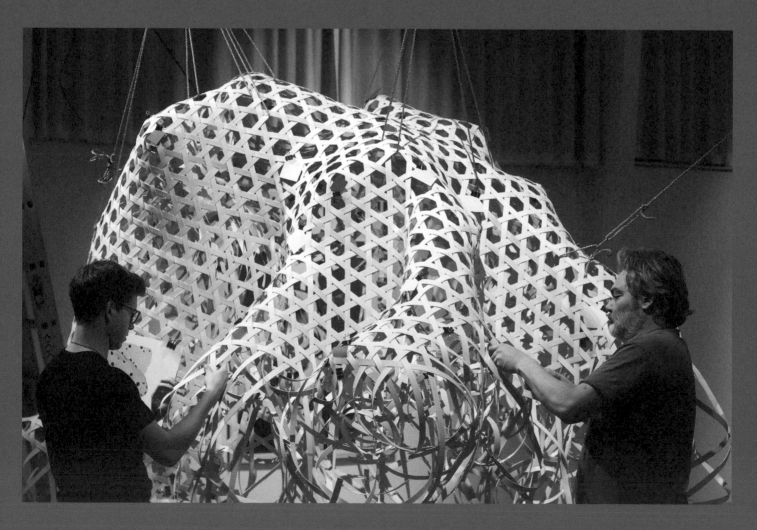

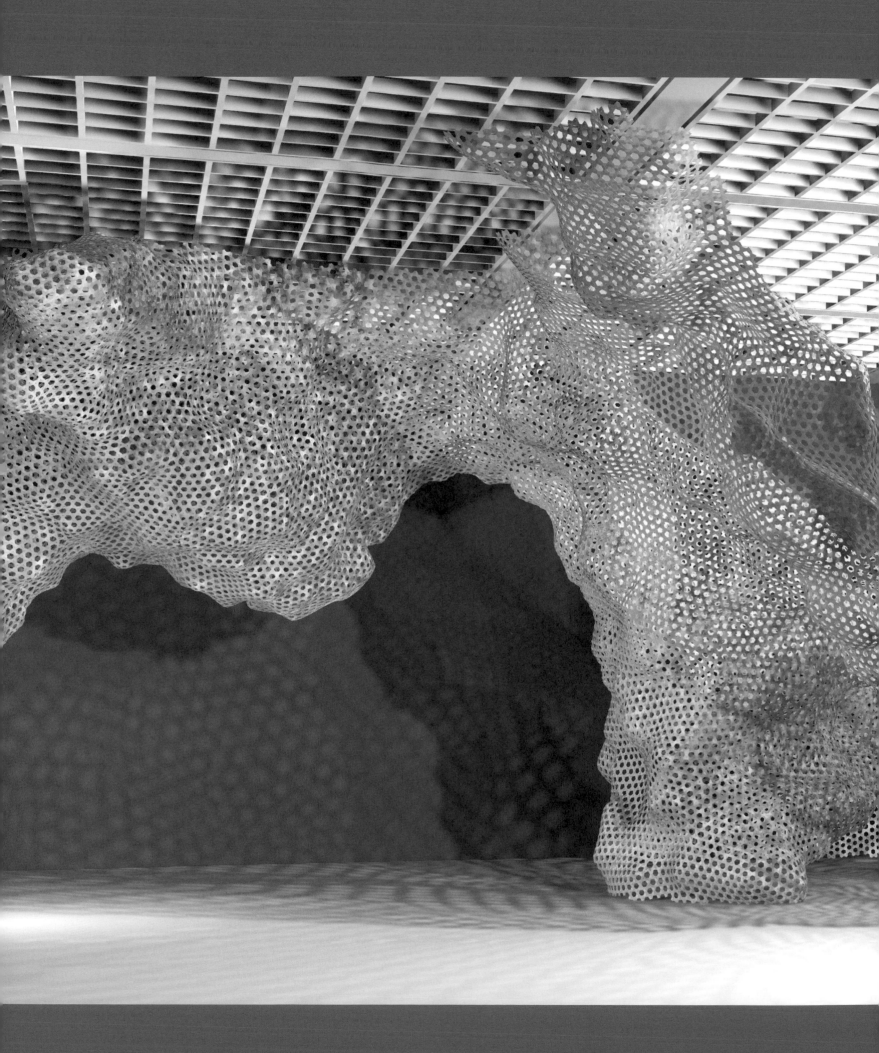

Towards a 21st Century Global African Art Museum

By Ngaire Blankenberg

Museums, the world over, have harmed Africans. One can argue even more strongly that many museums are synonymous with that harm, having been formed specifically to demonstrate evidence of sub-humanness that required intervention of missionaries, colonialists, industrialists and slave traders. Today, museums perpetuate that harm in erasing the connection between work, its source, the circumstances of removal and its meaning, by un-naming creators, ignoring community and making mistakes in documentation and interpretation.

Therefore, the museum as institution is up for a renegotiation, and rightly so. We can no longer accept the way, the institutions has used their cultural authority to minimise their role in the power structures. Let me use 'my own' museum as an example. Shortly after I joined the Smithsonian's National Museum of African Art (NMA-FA) in Washington D.C., US, in July 2021, we changed the foundation statements of the museum:

> Mission: To be a 21st century global African art museum
> Vision: To contribute to regenerative art ecosystems

The new mission and vision reflect our desire to imagine and create a new kind of art museum, one that responds to African art and African people in the context of today.

Our vision eschews the customary ambition to be 'the best' or the 'leading' but rather focusses on our role within a broader ecosystem in which we are only one player, working with others. We wish to contribute to creating something far more regenerative than the extractive practices of the colonial and neo-colonial forces that coercively took work away from its context and source, and even the capitalist art market of the past and present that buys and sells work for only the private enjoyment of the world's elite. Rather, we seek to contribute to an art ecosystem in Africa and the diaspora that supports artists to keep creating work to their fullest potential.

As an American national museum with a collection of African art that is being displayed, researched and cared for outside of Africa, largely by non-Africans, we do not have an inherent right to exist, regardless of the legal statutes and the federal subsidy that ensures that we do. We are profoundly grateful for that subsidy, which puts us in a financially stronger position than many museums and art centres across the continent and provides us with livelihoods more secure and generous than too many of our colleagues. It is precisely because of this privilege however that we are 'soul searching' to find a role for ourselves that is appropriate given our status, our location and our collection. Can we be considered legitimate if our existence is premised on the extraction of art from its source within a web of power that African artists and communities have been/are(?) excluded from?

This is not to say that this is the circumstance for most of our collection, it is not. Nevertheless, our vision of regenerative ecosystems reminds us to consider the power dynamics behind that which we have acquired (a collection of more than 12,000 works of art), what we gain from that 'ownership' (or stewardship) and what we have given and are giving back. It reminds us to consider the importance of equitable institutional collaboration; to acknowledge that African artists and their families and communities also need care (not just the works they produce); to support arts education, arts journalism and access for all as a way of ensuring a love for and the sustainability of arts on the continent; and to foreground our publics, their agency and our impact, alongside the more 'traditional' concerns of our own scholarship and work, and the priorities of collectors, donors and auction houses.

We are working towards centring African experiences and epistemologies, to build an institution 'for and of' Africa which creates space for and affirms the often trans-cultural, multi-dimensional experiences, identities and imaginations of African and African diasporic people and the art they create. Our goal is to be a 'trusted source' (a Smithsonian-wide priority) for everyone but especially for those who consider Africa at least one of their homes. Our legitimacy as 'authorities' on African art rests on the way in which we are perceived as trustworthy, fair and relevant by the people and communities from whom our work originates. We should only exist in a context of reciprocity and equitable exchange.

This means that issues of restitution are critically important. We need to attempt at least to repair the wrongs of history. Our recent restitution of twenty-nine Benin bronzes that had been in 'our' collection back to Nigeria demonstrates our commitment in that regard. Incidentally this commitment was first activated in 1973, when the museum's founder, Warren Robbins (1923-2008), restituted an Afo-A-Kom, sacred carved figure, that had been stolen in 1966, back to the Fon (King) of Kom in Cameroon.[1]

We are continuing to review the provenance of our collection, paying particular attention to the circumstances of removal, flagging objects we should not have and proactively reaching out to source nations and communities for their guidance. We are committed to continuing to work with these nations and communities to repair, if we can, the colonial violence we have participated in, if only by extension.

While our vision is our beacon for the future, our mission, albeit still aspirational, guides our everyday actions to get us there.

We chose the interdependent terms of 21st Century (to indicate a museum model of the now), Global African (to align with both the continent and the diaspora) and African Art (to consider the scope and form of what we present and collect) to provide the guidelines for a profound transformation.

Twenty-first century: a museum model of the now

When we speak of a twenty-first century museum, we are imagining a museum model that is not tied to the elite 'cabinets of curiosities' displaying trophies from the 'Age of Discovery' of sixteenth- and seventeenth-century Europe, nor the eighteenth- and nineteenth-century public museums of the West justifying the 'civilising' missions of war and colonialism and advancing European enlightenment values, nor even the nineteenth- and twentieth-century museum models of independence and postcolonialism, dedicated to nation building and science-based and technical education.

To develop a twenty-first-century museum model, we seek to contend with the impacts of twenty-first-century realities on what our museum is for and whom we serve. What is the role of our mu-

seum – as resources, as institution, as ideas and as physical infrastructure – in an era of machine learning, social media and mobiles;
voluntary migration and involuntary displacement; urbanisation;
cultural globalisation; hybrid and remote work; pandemics; inequality; diversity; xenophobia; terrorism; fragile and weak states; low-cost
travel; education crises; and extreme weather? What part do we play
in equipping our publics to face these opportunities and challenges?

These are big issues and of course no single museum can mitigate against hurricanes nor explosions, but could we be a place of
refuge, interpersonal connection and collaboration, celebration and
learning, for everyone and especially those whose imaginations and
even identities are looking for a home?

Global African: when the continent aligns with the diaspora
As a museum of African art located in a country with the second largest population of Africans outside of Africa (second to Brazil), most
of whom came here through acts of unimaginable violence over four
hundred years ago, but many who also came here less than twenty-
five years ago voluntarily, we connect with the complex, varied global
experience of Africans. As an American national institution born in
the 1970s, we are very much part of what the African Union identifies
as its sixth region[2] – the African diaspora.

When Warren Robbins, a former American Foreign Services
officer who had never been to Africa, established the Centre for
Cross-Cultural Understanding (CCC – the precursor of NMAFA)
in 1964 with collections he had bought from antique shops from
his time stationed in Germany, he did so with the goal of promoting
"better understanding between the peoples of different cultures."
He purchased the house of former abolitionist Frederick Douglass
(1818-1895) for the centre and identified three pillars on which the
centre would operate: "Inter-Disciplinarity, bringing together art
and social sciences accessible to the public; Inter-National, conversations and publishing between the United States and the world, and
Inter-Racial, creating opportunities for engagement between Black
and White Americans and Africans."[3]

Robbins felt strongly that by showcasing the rich cultures of

Africa in America the institute could challenge the notion that Black Americans were without a history. In addition to African work donated largely by diplomats and other private collectors, the museum also purchased work by African American artists, adding "the missing piece to a fully diasporic view of African art and its relation to African Americans."[4]

At the time of the CCC's inception, Washington, D.C. was the 'Black capital of America' – with Black people, almost entirely African American, forming almost 70 percent of its population.[5] Today, the Black population of D.C. has decreased and changed. More and more Black people have moved out of the cities – through the forces of suburbanisation (supported by a new highway) and gentrification. Today Black people make up about 45 percent of the population of D.C. Where the Black population was once almost all African American, it now boasts a significant number of more recent immigrants from Africa[6] mainly comprised of people from Ethiopia, Nigeria, Cameroon and Ghana.

Across the United States and the world, there are similar demographic changes. We recognise that today one fifth of Black people in the United States are immigrants or children of Black immigrants. And that more than half of Black immigrants arrived here in the United States after the year 2000[7] and were more likely to have a college degree than those born in the United States[8] – a stark change from centuries prior and even from when the museum was established. Given the fact that by 2025 more than half of the African population will be under twenty-five, and by 2050, one in four people on earth will be African, with Nigeria surpassing the United States as the third most populous country in the world, we can reasonably assume that in the coming years there will be more Africans not only in Africa but also in the world and most of them will be young. We can also assume that migration is not a one-way flow and identities are multifaceted. People go back and forth, one foot here and one foot there, a few years there, a few years here. There are intercultural unions, there is FaceTime and Zoom, remittances, travel, festivals, Years of Return,[9] collaboration.

This is the Global Africa we seek to locate ourselves among. As a national museum we are public, free and welcoming of everyone. However, as demographics of the world and our communities shift, so do we. We do not need to *explain* Africa to Americans. Africans *are* Americans and increasingly so. Young Global Africans, our target audience, are our bellwether for what is to come – in the United States and in the world.

African art: the scope and the form

Unlike many of the European ethnographic museums that have become world culture or art museums, the National Museum of African Art has always been an art museum. In the 1960s and 1970s, recognising African art as art within an art canon defined by the West was a decision by a smattering of museums across the world of which the National Museum of African Art was one. It was at the time a bold statement in an environment in which African art was often stereotyped to 'song and dance' or 'craft and heritage' and the only form of African art sold on auction was described as 'primitive' or 'tribal.'

The 'battle' for recognition among Western art historians has now been 'won,' with African art now a bona fide discipline in its own right at Western universities across the world. But now we are turning our attention to legitimacy within an African context – somehow overlooked in the rush for legitimacy of the 'Academy.' What is African art as defined by Africans?

We aim to (re)root African art at NMAFA within African systems of thought, to consider African art in a broader context than aesthetics and materials. We aim to find ways to understand African art as a language in and of itself of African philosophy and African cosmology. African art as living ideas. We explore the intersections among creators, the contexts of creation (spiritual as well as historical and geographic), the identities and influences of the translators (museums, gallerists, collectors, writers) and the meaning and impact of the work on today's publics.

Our new foundation statements articulate an aspiration to evolve our position, relationships and activities in the world. We do not know exactly where we will end up, nor exactly how to get there. We are embarking on a journey into the unknown (but not the unknowable) – with all the exhilaration and the anxiety that journeys into the unknown entail. We know we can't do it alone. We are inviting many people in to help us think through these things – from African architects and designers who helped us to develop design principles as we review our physical spaces, to branding and communication consultants, to scholars and thinkers (through our Scholarly Advisory Committee), to community influencers and mobilisers (through our Glo-cal Advisory Committee), to students, local artists and creatives and more. Our museum of the future must be an open, ever-evolving project.

Repair

Our experiments in how to develop 'African art experiences' begin but do not end with repair. After the restitution of twenty-nine works of Royal Court Art (referred to as the Benin bronzes in our collection) back to Nigeria, we are now collaborating with Nigeria's National Commission of Museums and Monuments (NCMM) on a multi-pronged project that will place the returned bronzes in conversation with contemporary creation. Together, a team of Edo and Nigerian curators, researchers, designers, writers, artists, content creators, web developers, educators and so on (some hired by us as contractors and others by the NCMM) are developing a five part exhibition and parallel programmes partly co-created by local communities in Benin City. The goal is to benefit local artists and museum professionals through commissions, contracts, skills development opportunities and/or recognition.

Through the blessing and involvement of local healers (teachers, spiritual healers, mental health professionals), we are working to find ways to ensure the returned art also has maximum positive impact on local people – particularly in relation to collective well-being, pride and self-esteem. This group of advisors will determine what positive impact looks like and how to measure it.

Although every instance is unique, we hope to learn from this experience, share it more broadly and re-apply what makes sense in subsequent collaborations resulting from transfers of ownership and/or voluntary shared stewardship.

Dealing with race

At its inception in 1964, the Museum of African Art's primary aim was to address racism in the United States and beyond. Although Robbins, as a white Jewish man at the helm of this endeavour, was met with a certain amount of skepticism by African American leaders in Washington, D.C.,[10] and Robbins himself refused to acknowledge how his own subjectivities impacted his actions,[11] the museum did not shy away from race and racism.

Since then, however, the museum has barely touched on issues of race – the quintessential issue that created the diaspora – and that continues to be central to the lives of people of African descent in the Americas and Europe. In fact, when the museum gave its collection of work by African Americans to the Smithsonian American Art Museum, it arguably divested itself of the responsibility of 'dealing with race' – a concern primarily of diasporic peoples which had become 'out of scope' for the museum. This became even easier with the development of the National Museum of African American History and Culture – established by an Act of Congress in 2003 and open to the public in 2016, with a mandate to tell the American story through the lens of African American history and culture.

With another museum volunteering to take on the messiness of race in America, the National Museum of African Art has focussed on presenting African art on a continuum – from the eleventh century (where our collection starts) to contemporary commissions – without it being defined by the colonial moment. It sought to accept African art on its own terms and for its own sake – not instrumentalised for a broader purpose (such as Robbins' cross-culturalism).

This approach continues to be fundamental to the work of the museum. The enormous breadth of our collection (across time but also including works from forty-eight African countries) gives us a unique opportunity to put different eras, countries, media in dialogue and conversation with one another.

BUT the place where we live is still fraught with issues of race and racism.

The museum was formed during the civil rights era in a city and country with deep racial tensions.[12] Today, racial inequities and inter-generational racial trauma persist and, in some cases, increase all around us.[13] Our commitment to the global African cause and the entanglements of life in the twenty-first century propels us to make space for the issues of racialisation. We believe in the power of art – to soothe, to inspire, to galvanise, to critique – whether through exhibition, public programmes or publications. In this moment, we do not want to shy away from the racism and trauma that systemic and inter-personal racism causes and has caused (in and through the work and lives of artists), nor the joy, resilience or creativity of global Blackness.

Space and place
The majority (96 percent) of our 117,000-square-feet museum is underground. It forms part of a larger 'quadrangle complex' designed in 1982 by French architect Jean Paul Carlhain (1919-2012), with the contributions of several architects including Japanese architect Junzō Yoshimura (1908-1997), who developed the idea of a build-ing under a garden. This concept was hugely challenging to execute as one third of the complex sits below the city's water table. It is a display of remarkable hubris. Other than the entrance pavilion, and one 2,000-square-feet gallery on the first sublevel, all of the exhibi-tion, programme and staff spaces have no access to natural light or, mostly, cell phone reception. Although situated visibly on a main road in Washington, D.C. (Independence Avenue), it is complete-ly invisible from 'the mall' – that emblematic stretch of land from the Washington Monument to the Capitol onto which eleven out of twenty-one of our sister museums overlook and from where most visitors come.

How can we turn this barely visible, sublevel museum into a space for who we, as an institution and a public, are becoming? We can imagine our museum as a kind of cave – a place that Cave_bureau reminds us is nature's manifestation of a museum – places where billions of years of planetary and human cultures and histories are layered into the rocky walls. Except everything about our museum is (white) man-made and its thirty-five-year history is a tiny, tiny blip in time; we still like the analogy.

I sometimes also imagine our museum is morphing into the American activists and scholars Fred Moten (born 1962) and Stefano Harney's (born 1962) 'undercommons' – places of anti-establishmentarianism, resistance and wild fugitive community. A literal and metaphorical underground, except, we are a national museum, part of a 'trust instrumentality of the United States, created by Congress in 1846 to exercise the authority of the United States over the Smithsonian's original bequest. Our highest authority is the establishment itself – a board of regents consisting of the chief justice, the vice president, three members of the Senate, three members of the House of Representatives, and nine citizen members appointed by a joint resolution of Congress. Does rebellion from the centre mean the margins are co-opted?

In early 2022 we convened a group of African advisors to help us reimagine our spaces. These included Cave_bureau's Kabage Karanja and Stella Mutegi, but also Sumayya Vally from counterspace, Emmanuel Admassu from AD-WO, Farida Abu-Bakare from WXY architecture + urban design, Satyajit Das from Architecture Social Club, Rowland Abíodún (Professor of Art History and Black Studies, Amherst College), Jay Pather (Director of Institute for Creative Arts, South Africa) and Nkiru Nzegwu (SUNY Distinguished Professor of Africana Studies and Women, Gender and Sexuality Studies at State University of New York, Binghamton).

Together, we discussed the possibilities of a 21st Century Global African Art Museum and developed a set of design principles to guide future spatial design – whether architecture, exhibition or interior design.

Design Principles towards a 21st Century Global African Art Museum

Repair: Use the built environment to contribute to healing and repair of individuals, communities and society. Be honest about the past – 'keep the void' – allow spaces of silence. Repair from harmful museological/ethnographic practices – theft, erasure, misinterpretation, marginalisation. Build trust.

Intactness: Restore the image and experience of African art to one that includes context, community, place; that shows the 'whole' picture on African terms (the spirit world, the community, the materials). Shift from Eurocentric view of what is 'whole.'

Plurality: Celebrate plurality in forms, disciplines, modes of engagement (reflective, celebratory), pace (fast and slow), scale (from micro to macro), environments (light, dark, noisy, quiet). Reject Eurocentric separation and hierarchical classification.

Hybridity: Include mixedness not just multiple separates – of people, places and forms. Art is not separate and isolated but is often hybrid, pan, mixed – as is the Trans-Atlantic experience.

Imagination: Emphasise agency and imagination. Imagination as an act of liberation. Allow people to lose themselves in the art, to unleash their own imaginations.

Imperfection: Allow for imperfections and iterations, transparency. Challenge the snobbery of perfection – by whose eyes?

Disruption: Play with legibility and illegibility – expected and unexpected. Encourage going beyond and looking again. Disrupt hegemony, support critical thinking, create unusual juxtapositions, unexpected experiences. Challenge and disrupt harmful norms.

Bio-integrative, regenerative: Integrate and regenerate living matter – of place, of surrounding, of people. Connect nature and natural materials to the interior experience. African Indigenous knowledge systems; challenge extractive practices, alienation from natural resources.

Alive: Consider objects and building as alive, play with texture, motion, sound, light, smell. African epistemologies support living objects, bringing together of material and immaterial worlds, animism.

Belonging: Create spaces of belonging for global Africans, remove barriers and discomfort. Museum as a comfortable place for global Africans.

Recognition/presence: Moments of recognition for global Africans – in the form (home/shrine/marketplace/cafe), in the content, in the interactions. I see you. Elements of familiarity.

Communities/collaboration: Support trans-local communities, 'support structures for support structures'. Support co-working, collaborating. Create spaces of belonging of being together.

We are working through these bit by bit. We launched our Research Gallery in February 2023 – a space for creative incubation, community and co-working and are working to repair our relationship with the artistic communities of Washington, D.C., Maryland and Virginia where we are located to ensure we provide a free and accessible place for thinking about, researching and creating art. We are programming community mixers 'crits' and masterclasses, calls for curators and designers and more.

Our new digital gallery, we refer to as 'the Void,' is inspired by our brief encounters with Kabage Karanja and Stella Mutegi and their manifesto in which the void is the city of neglected slums, informal settlements out of municipal control; it will bisect the three layers of the museum, disrupting the flow of the building. Taking the form of a black hole or cylinder, the scale and presence of the Void is being designed to deliberately contradict the idea of 'invisibility' or 'non-being'. The structure is a symbol that boldly refutes the attempted erasure and neglect of African peoples, epistemologies and cultures by colonial violence. Projected on the structure 'outside, inside' will be digital art, or in more art museum parlance 'time-based media work' – work that records live art, or that exists as pixels, light flows, movement – elusive but powerful.

We imagine our Void as a space from which art, imagination, thought and meaning emerges and descends, a space of reclamation through artistic 'phygital' hybrid forms that defy categorisation, disrupt assumptions and affirm the dynamic, living pulses of African creativity.[14]

We have kept the blank spaces where the Benin bronzes used to be – allowing uncomfortable interruptions in the otherwise seamlessly designed permanent gallery. Our vestibule space is being re-designed for meditation and reflection with a lighting rig that can just easily transform it to a bubble of elation and joy.

Presence through trans-localism
The twenty-first century is marked by both the rise in 'affordable' air travel enabling greater movement of people than ever before, to and from Africa, and the rise in high-speed internet and video calling,

enticing people to not move at all. Museum visitation has soared, and then subsided due to attention migrating to the internet and then the pandemic. Like most museums, we are also thinking about how to navigate presence in the post-pandemic, digital, travel, protectionist age. We believe there is still value in real life – people talking to one another in person, people seeing the 'real' work – as much as there is value in the unmooring enabled by digital and the mobile phone.

Our experiment now is with 'trans-localism' – a strategy to be rooted locally in a lot of places, while also being a space on the internet, and/or metaverse. Our NMAFA+ programme is about having a presence across the United States, on the continent and in the diaspora. We are experimenting with a form in which we start with a short-term exhibition in partnership with a local institution, curated by a local curator, with commissions from local artists. These 'pop-up' exhibitions are accompanied by a talks programme (African Artists Host Conversations) as well as city tours 'through the eyes of artists' connecting art with place.

NMAFA+ aims to seed collaborations. If it goes well, we continue to grow the collaboration to a more long-term partnership in which we begin to share collections taking on the work of international loan agreements and visas not just between us at NMAFA and our partner, but, the vision goes, among all the network of partners.

Interrogating museum professionalism and expertise

When the Museum of African Art became the Smithsonian Museum of African Art in 1987, it also became a 'professional' museum driven by scholarly research rather than the community 'museum that communicates' of the Centre for Cross-Cultural Understanding.[15] This shift coincided with a rapid professionalisation of the study and presentation of African art that took place in the United States and European academic institutions and museums during the 1980s. We are now run to the highest standards of museum professionalism, but what does that mean and how do these standards affirm and regenerate?

The process of professionalisation is a double-edged sword. On the one hand, standards of practice give guidelines for people to be able to care for and keep track of collections. They enable museums to talk to one another, to loan work and exhibitions and to facilitate research.

On the other hand, the museums of today reflect European enlightenment values of 'measurement, classification and knowing' as well as hierarchies in which Western/European knowledge[16] is at the top. Museum standards, informed by Western distinctions between science and spirit, and Western values of what is to be preserved, valued, documented and how, have long been a way to continue the separation of African peoples with work that has originated with them. Western museum professionalism can remove knowhow from its context, and create a situation where professional bodies in Paris, for example, dictate standards of care for Abidjan.

This has had dire consequences for Africa, where claims for restitution have been rebuffed through the 'professional standards' argument most commonly in relation to collections management and care.[17] African museums or cultural centres or community places that do not have adequate climate control, shelving or locked doors have been deemed as not 'ready' to take (re)possession of their work. Yet many, many communities have employed Indigenous methods of care successfully for centuries – ensuring valuable heritage can be passed down by generations.

'Professionalisation' can also hide individual bias. It can give the illusion that museological practices are 'neutral,' separated from the ideologies shaping them, and separate from the subjectivities of the person who enacts them. We can believe that there is a 'right' way and a 'wrong' way to do museums, ignoring diverse ways race, ethnicity, and culture are experienced, debated and practiced even at work.

There is a lack of diversity in the people who work in museums and art history academies. In art museum leadership positions in the United States, only 12 percent are people of colour,[18] amongst museum curators, only 16 percent and speaking at in conversation events, 11 percent. The museum profession overall in the United States is one of the least diverse – with 6 percent of archivists, curators and museum technicians being Black or African American.[19] Typical 'feeders' into art museum are university art history departments

– yet in the United States, 7 percent of professors of art history are Black or African American. Why are there so few African and African diasporic peoples getting paid to care for, document, research, exhibit African art? What is lost when we remove personal connection from professional practice? We have been blessed with a staff who are dedicated and passionate, but we can do more. We need to check ourselves. Is our loyalty to our learned professionalism creating blinders when it comes to really seeing what the work itself is asking to be?

Knowledge production – African Museology

With our three-year African Museology project we are reassessing protocols of care (handling, storage, conservation treatment); documentation in the database, archives and conservation lab; and collections research. We are working towards a new method and language of doing museums.

We have brought together African scholars, thinkers and doers to co-develop an approach or framework for collections management and research that centres African Indigenous knowledge systems and values. This requires a process of un-learning and re-learning, which we will do alongside a cohort of eight cultural heritage practitioners from Ethiopia, Mali, DR Congo, Nigeria, Tanzania, Kenya, Rwanda and South Africa. We imagine the framework as guidelines, principles or approaches that we will then apply to eight pilot projects led by our collaborators. Each of the pilot project has their own aim unique to their particular contexts and collections, however we hope that these will also surface common challenges and approaches, helpful for one another.

The universal of horizon or translation[20]

Our fundamental shift when it comes to knowledge production, is that we do not know it all. We are proud of the work we have done to understand the work in our collection and what it says about the creators and contexts of creation; and we are proud of our efforts over the years to share these with a diverse public. But we also know that our knowledge has limits. Despite PhDs and combined decades of

Notes

1 Thomas A. Johnson, "Afo-A-Kom Joyously Greeted on Its Return Home," *New York Times*, 14 December 1973, https://www.nytimes.com/1973/12/14/archives/afoakom-joyously-greeted-on-its-return-home-afoa-komis-joyously.html.

2 'Diaspora' is defined by the African Union as "those irrespective of citizenship and nationality who are willing to contribute to the development of the continent [. . .]." "The Diaspora Division," African Union, https://au.int/en/diaspora-division.

3 Steve Nelson, "The Museum of African Art and African American Art in 1960s Washington," in *Beauty Born of Struggle: The Art of Black Washington*, ed. Jeffrey C. Stewart (National Gallery of Art/Yale University Press, 2023), 6.

4 Nelson, 14.

5 In the 1970 census, the population of "Negros" in Washington, D.C. was 71.1 percent. David Rusk, "Goodbye to Chocolate City," D.C. Policy Center, 20 July 2017, https://www.dcpolicycenter.org/publications/goodbye-to-chocolate-city/.

6 In 2011, for the first time, D.C.'s Black population fell below fifty percent as a result of suburbanisation, supported by federal highway construction and gentrification. Today the Black population of D.C. is about forty-five. About one in seven of the total population are immigrants, with people from Ethiopia being the second largest immigrant group (second to El Salvador) and Washington, D.C. being the city with the third highest number of Black immigrants in the United States. lytics-lab/structural-racism-explainer-collection/combating-legacy-segregation-nations-capital, retrieved March 2023. 'Number of black D.C. residents plummets as majority status slips away,' Carol Morello and Dan Keating, 24 March, 2011,

Washington Post https://www.washingtonpost.com/local/black-dc-residents-plummet-barely-a-majority/2011/03/24/ABtIgJQB_story.html; *Key findings about Black immigrants in the U.S.*, Christine Tamir, Pew Research Center, 27 January 2022. https://www.pewresearch.org/fact-tank/2022/01/27/key-findings-about-black-immigrants-in-the-u-s/; Immigrants in the District of Columbia, State by State, 6 August 2020, American Immigration Council https://www.americanimmigrationcouncil.org/research/immigrants-in-washington-dc#:~:text=One%20in%20seven%20D.C.%20residents,14%20percent%20of%20the%20population.

7 Pew Research Center, "Key findings about Black immigrants in the US."

8 Pew Research Center, "Key findings about Black immigrants in the US."

9 A campaign to encourage African Americans to move to/visit Ghana spearheaded by the Ghana Tourism Authority (GTA) under the auspices of the Ministry of Tourism, Arts and Culture in collaboration with the Office of Diaspora Affairs at the Office of the President the PANAFEST Foundation and the Adinkra Group of the USA. https://www.yearofreturn.com/.

10 Nelson, 14.

11 Robbins allegedly responded to some questions or complaints that he was a white man operating a museum of African art: "I make no apologies for being white. You

Ngaire Blankenberg, director of the Smithsonian's National Museum of African Art in Washington, D.C., US, 2021-2023.

study and experience, we have much to learn. This is hard to admit – collaboration requires humility and patience. We are used to wearing our professionalisms as shields and swords.

Developing equitable contracts and memorandums of understanding with many different people in different countries tax our bureaucratic systems, communicating across time-zones and geographies requires new working hours and new technologies which have been facilitated but are still far from perfect; recognising wisdom outside of books, articles and presentations, fluent language but in bodies, silences, proverbs and art itself requires space and time.

We want to get better at translation, that which the Senegalese philosopher Souleymane Bachir Diagne (born 1955) calls the 'creation of reciprocity'. For a museum such as ours, with the multitude of languages it contains, we cannot say anything that is not understood at least in part, in translation. We aspire to a 'lateral' nor a hierarchical universal[21] in which, through translation, cultures and people are in constant dialogue with one another. We will never get to one dominant meaning but may arrive at a constellation of meanings that are mutually understood. That is good enough.

We need to figure out the conversations – not just between an essential Africa and America – but among Africans. How can we begin the mammoth work of translation and interpretation that our collection encourages?

We are busy. We are thinking. We are evolving. We are making mistakes. Our museum of the present and of the future is not fixed. It is fluid and flawed, but we are hopeful.

don't have to be Chinese to appreciate ancient ceramics, and you don't have to be a fish to be an ichthyologist." Joe Holley, "Warren M. Robbins, founder of the Museum of African Art, dies at 85," *Los Angeles Times*, 8 December 2008, https://www.latimes.com/local/obituaries/lame-robbins8-2008dec-08story.html#:~:text=You%20don't%20have%20to,fish%20to%20be%20an%20ich-thyologist.%E2%80%9D&-text=When%20the%20museum%20had%20ex-panded,Institution%2C%20which%20happened%20in%201979.

12 In the1960s, the vast majority of the police force in D.C. was white, policing a majority Black city. In June 1967, the national unemployment rate was 4 percent for white Americans and 8.4 percent for non-white Americans. In D.C., non-white unemployment was over 30 percent for much of the 1960s, many times higher than national rates. *Algernon Austin, The Unfinished March: An Overview Report,* Economic Policy Institute,18 June 2013, https://www.epi.org/publication/unfinished-march-over-view/#:~:text=In%201963%2C%20the%20unem-ployment%20rate,the%20white%20rate%2C%20for%20blacks.3

13 Despite continued economic growth, there are ongoing racialised disparities in housing, health, wealth, employment and education in D.C. and in America. "Racial Equity in D.C.," D.C. Policy Center,

https://www.dcpolicycenter.org/racialequity/.

14 Concept note from the Void, developed December 2022.

15 Nelson, 14.

16 Emmanuel Chukwudi Eze ed., *Race and the Enlightenment: A Reader* (Wiley-Blackwell, 1997).

17 Bénédicte Savoy, *Africa's Struggle for Its Art: History of a Postcolonial Defeat,* trans. Susanne Meyer-Abich (Princeton University Press, 2022).

18 Association of Art Museum Directors, *Latest Art Museum Staff Demographic Survey Shows Number of African American Curators and Women in Leadership Roles Increased*, 28 January 2019, https://www.aam-us.org/2019/01/28/latest-art-museum-staff-de-mographic-survey-shows-in-creases-in-african-amer-ican-curators-and-wom-en-in-leadership-roles/.

19 U.S. Bureau of *Labour Statistics, Labor Force Statistics from the Current Population Survey*, https://www.bls.gov/cps/cpsaat11.htm.

20 Souleymane Bachir Diagne, "No Civilisation is an Island," Sciences Po, 28 September 2021, https://www.sciencespo.fr/en/news/souleymane-ba-chir-diagne-no-civilisa-tion-is-an-island-1.

21 Diagne, "No Civilisation is an Island."

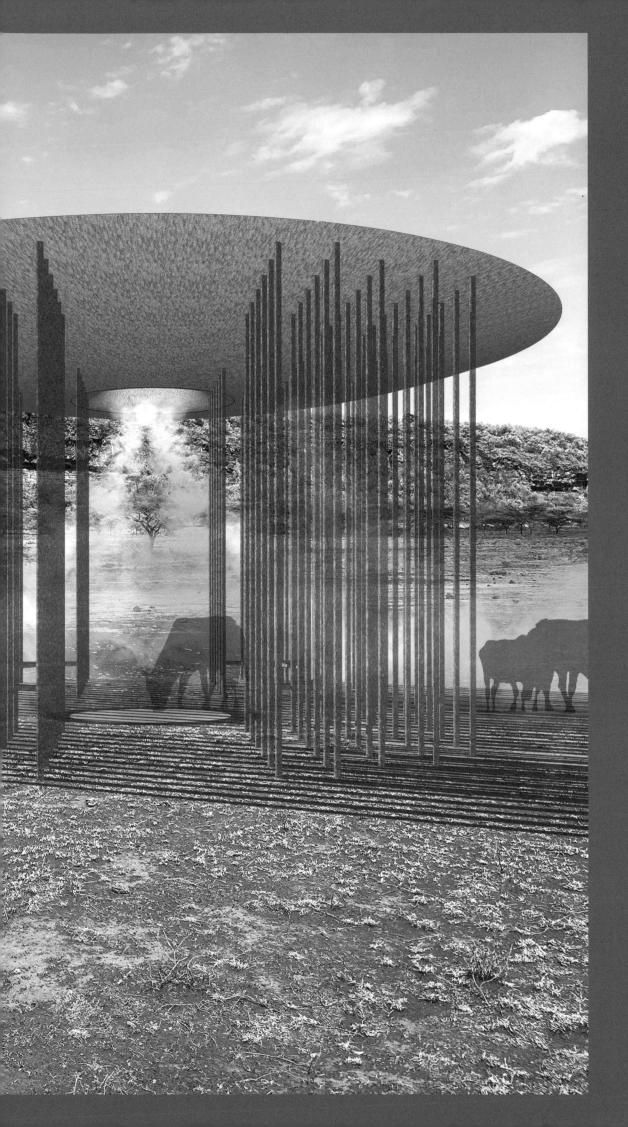

Nyukie Artefact, Steam Harvester

Exacerbated by climate change, the frequency and severity of droughts experienced by the Maasai community on Mount Suswa in Kenya and across the region has reached a critical point. On top of this, the Kenyan government's appetite to expand on the exploitation of geothermal energy along this corridor has proven to be significantly detrimental to the natural environment and community rights. This project looks to reimagine infrastructural devices that address the unsustainable practices of geothermal energy extraction in the Great Rift Valley. The Nyukie artefact, inspired by successful makeshift Maasai solutions to harvest water from the natural geothermal vents, is an optimised device that condenses and collects water for drinking and watering cows and crops, especially during droughts. The project is the first iteration of the design intended to be deployed in Suswa and other volcanically active sites along the Great Rift Valley. Using the expertise of volcanologists and mechanical engineers, geologists and hydrologists, the project is a working prototype that acts as both a steam and rainwater harvester, but more importantly as a community condenser where both humans and non-humans can commune beneath the reservoir that is scalable on a broader infrastructural network of existence.

It also taps into the Maasai people's monotheistic faith in the God they call Engai, who is mostly benevolent and who manifests in the form of different colours, according to his feelings. The changing colours and movements of the filaments across the steam harvester signal the mountain's temperament and its connection to a higher power. A geological and spiritual register of a complex planetary system at work.

Anthropocene Museum 8.0: *Nyukie Artefact*, *Steam Harvester*, Mount Suswa, Kenya, 2023. Steam Harvester.

Cave_bureau, collages and drawing. Mapping of the geothermal energy extraction projects in Olkaria, Naivasha, Kenya, where multiple international agencies and investment organisation oversaw the gross displacement of the Maasai community and damage to the natural ecosystems.
Architectural studies to reimagine geothermal extractions which are aligned with the Maasai's community's way of life and in harmony with the natural environment.

W di Caves of Sharjah

The Anthropocene Museum 9.0

The Wadi Caves of Sharjah stretch across the Meliha Mountains, a range that forms part of a network of geological formations registered as a UNESCO World Heritage site. These were rock shelters dating as far back as the early Stone Age, Palaeolithic time, where one of the earliest evidences of modern human life outside Africa was found.

The Al Faya Cave 1.0 located on the Eastern slopes of the Meliha Mountains is where a stone axe dating as far back as 125,000 years was found. It is believed that the site was used as an elevated place of shelter overlooking the hunting plains beneath, amongst other modes of early human habitation. It is a site where early humans contemplated ways to find, catch, consume and process food to cater for their sustenance on this planet.

Using our Cave_bureau methodology, we scanned the cave in three dimensions to create an installation for the Sharjah Architecture Triennial 2023. The old Sharjah slaughterhouse, located in the city centre, is our focus. It is akin to the Al Faya Cave site, except today such buildings are completely dislocated from our consciousness. How we source and process our food has become a dislocated process of anthropogenic proportions where livestock have become the most populous mammal species on earth. Revisiting both sites is a return to a state of origin from whence we transgressed.

Anthropocene Museum 9.0: *Wadi Caves of Sharjah*, Sharjah Architecture Triennal, 2023–2024. Cave register.

Cave_bureau, collage and drawing. A cross section of the Meliha Mountain range featuring the Al Faya cave, which is set in a cove, reducing exposure to the elements. The sketches explore how transposing the geometry of the cave produces new possible functions.

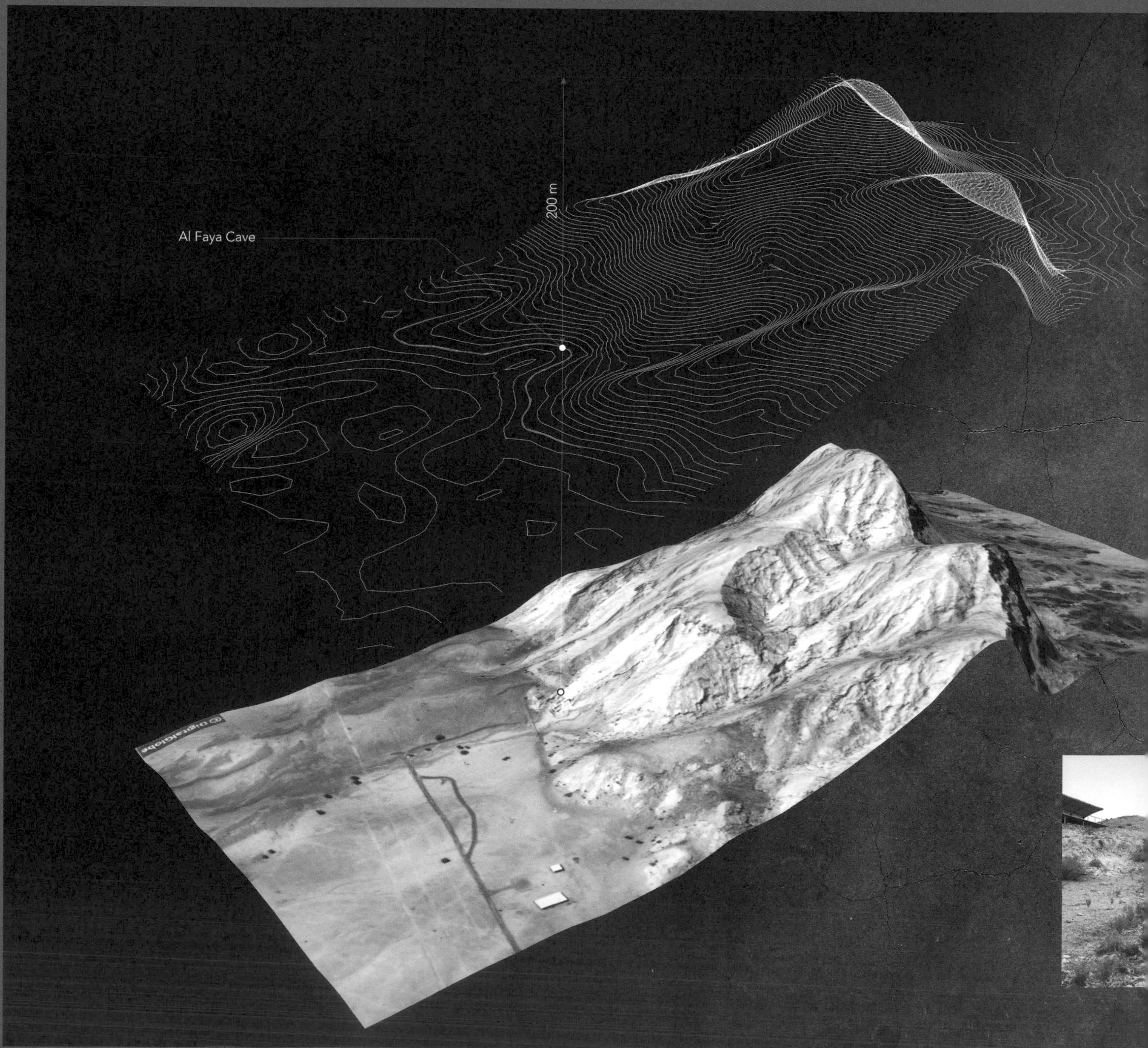

Al Faya Cave

200 m

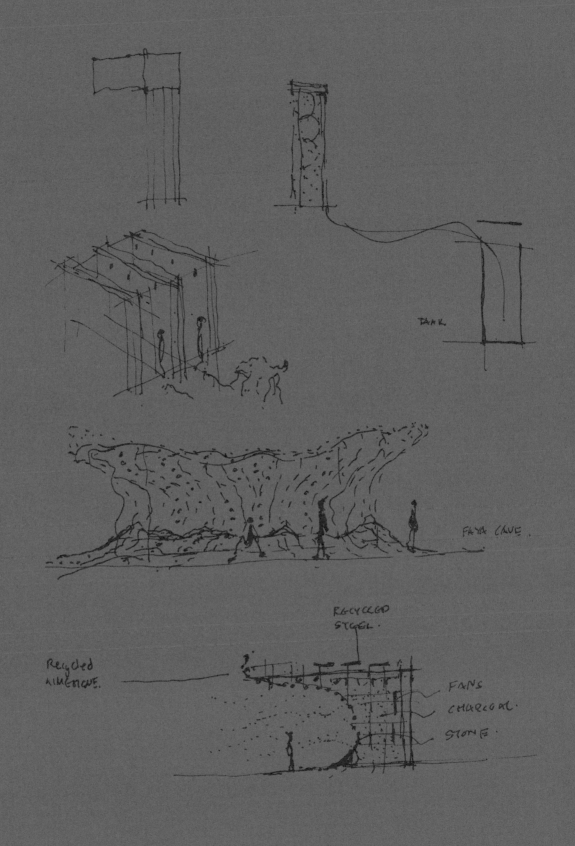

TANK

FAYA CAVE.

Recycled
LIMESTONE.

RECYCLED
STEEL.

FANS
CHARCOAL.
STONE.

Cave_bureau, map and collages. 60 percent of all mammals are livestock, with humans making up 0.01 percent of biomass on Earth, even though we have wiped out 83 percent of all wild mammals. Over time the human species have managed to cut the global biomass by half. The map shows the global spread of livestock on the planet. While the thumbnail images depict Cave_bureau's Sharjah slaughterhouse tour sequence, which was made for the Sharjah Triennale, 2023.

That Rug Has to Go

A conversation between Lesley Lokko,
Kabage Karanja and Stella Mutegi

KABAGE KARANJA Your *White Papers, Black Marks: Architecture, Race, Culture* is a pivotal book of reference and grounding for our work here at Cave_bureau, as it obviously has been for many people and practices around the world. It was published in year 2000, the same year as Paul Crutzen and Eugene Stormer [an atmospheric chemist and limnologist, respectively.] coined the term 'Anthropocene.' For us this is no coincidence, when thinking about how fresh and yet critical these ideas of architecture, race and culture were at that time. What are your thoughts when considering how this and your subsequent works have played a critical role in expanding the more challenging discourse surrounding this so-called age of the human?

LESLEY LOKKO For some reason, the term 'Anthropocene' wasn't on my radar around the time I was finishing at the Bartlett [School of Architecture, University College London], which is when I started thinking about *White Papers, Black Marks*. Maybe I wasn't reading the right texts, but it wasn't until a good ten years later that I heard the term. It always remains slightly ambiguous for me because I felt like I'd come to an understanding of it quite late. My starting point for *White Papers, Black Marks*, like with many Black and African students, was deeply personal. I kept hearing the word culture. "Culture, culture, culture." They were talking about culture at the Bartlett, it was on everybody's lips. But I couldn't connect the way people there were thinking about culture to the way I understood it.

For me, it was the first inkling that there was a mismatch between what I thought and what I was being taught, but I wasn't sophisticated enough in my understanding to realise that the deficit wasn't me.

So for the first three or four years, I thought, crudely, "I'm the problem. I'm not getting it."

And then a book on architecture and gender came out, it was Francesca Hughes's *The Architect: Reconstructing Her Practice* (1996). And I came to architecture quite late, I was a mature student, so she was actually younger than me. And I remember thinking, 'If somebody who is younger than me can publish a book about gender and architecture, *me too*, I can publish a book about race.'

White Papers, Black Marks was actually born out of a desire to find out if other people around the world were thinking, if not in similar ways, at least on the same topic. Now, in retrospect, I realise I was looking for validation for ideas. Not from my immediate tutors, because none of them could give it, but I had to go out and find another community that was thinking about it in the same way. And when I started getting the essays together, I essentially copied what someone else had done and I looked at *The Architect: Reconstructing Her Practice*, I looked at another few anthologies, and I thought, "Okay, this is the format." It was super clear to me even then that many African and diasporic practitioners were actually thinking about race in very different ways. So I think I started out thinking there was going to be one answer, and in the end, came to understand that it's almost infinite, which was a real liberation. You didn't have to have an answer to a problem. This was actually just a field that you could start to explore. Thirty years later, I would say that your work is very much part of that trajectory of exploration.

Unravelling architecture

KK What struck us when thinking about the

Anthropocene was how important it is to initiate a cultural and more-than-human interrogation by asking: the Anthropocene *for* who? *By* who, and when did it even begin in the first place? We began to question and unravel the term, and for us it has been really liberating. And I guess, in a way, our methods and thoughts can be considered as – maybe unintended – consequences of what you began with your work. What are your current thoughts on the field?

LL For me, questions of race and identity and resources in connection with climate change, environmental justice, social justice, they're two sides of the same coin. I always say that Black bodies were Europe's first units of energy. So there's been a relationship between labour, body, race and environment since time immemorial. This is just another iteration of a millennia-year-old dynamic.

I remember the very first public lecture I gave, it was at the Prince of Wales's Institute in London, which is quite a strange place to talk about race and architecture. I was very, very nervous, and about 20 minutes into the talk, a man came into the room and switched on the lights. He was a Black British guy dressed in an old-fashioned English gentleman's suit, quite strange looking in a way. He said in a very posh English voice: "Young lady, do you mind if I interrupt?" I'm like: "Okay?" And so he says: "I have been listening to you for about twenty minutes, you were talking about race and architecture, and I have a few questions for you." I needed to finish the lecture, so I was like, "Oh God, where are we going here?" And everybody was looking, because it's not normal protocol. And he says: "Do you know where the term opera comes from? Well, the form that we call opera today was reconstructed out of fragments of history."

There was an art form that existed before the fall of classical Greece, but no one really captured what it was. You have reference to this art practice in historical documents, but not to the full description. In the Renaissance, there was a deliberate attempt to recreate something from the bits and pieces that they had. And the thing that they recreated is what we call opera today. But it's not an authentic art form, it's a reconstructed art form.

"So," he says, "the question I have for you is, if you put these two terms, race and architecture, together, are you prepared to accept that what you will get at the end of your investigation will neither be exactly race nor architecture? In other words, are you prepared to accept that your investigation will undo architecture as you understand it?"

It was quite a difficult question to answer thirty years ago. And it turned out that he was the first Black British PhD in musicology at Oxford University. So the history of music was his thing. It's a question that's always stayed with me, because if you do pursue these questions of race, identity, resource, power, language, translation, diaspora, what you essentially do is you unravel all of the things that holds architecture together: something fixed in a location, it's made out of a certain form, it has certain precedence, it has certain tectonics. But as you say, even with the Anthropocene, these things that hold it together, come from somewhere. They didn't arrive from nowhere. So those of us who critique the term, actually we're critiquing the thing itself.

I can see this in your work. A lot of people are agitated about your work, asking questions like, "Is it architecture?" The usual stuff. And my answer to this is, that questioning is the starting point for you to not accept everything that's been handed to you. It might be uncomfortable because nobody likes to have the rug pulled from under their feet, but in order to reimagine a new way of thinking about architecture, that rug has to go.

So what I really enjoy about your work, for example, is that you use the tools of seduction, of beauty, of imagination, of creativity, of speculation to really dismantle the thing. But you dismantle it in its own terms. And that makes people very agitated because, on the one hand, you come to the drawings or to the models or to the thinking, and you think that you understand what it is, but it's like the scorpion. As soon as you go into it, tail comes up, bang, sting! And the sting will kill you. It'll kill architecture. But so gently. It'll die slowly. That, for me, is really interesting about seeing this newer generation of thinkers and makers and doers emerging, who are not afraid to use the tools of architecture in myriad ways, which I think my generation were; always questioning "how am I going to make a living, how am I going to survive," which was stopping us.

Translating worlds

LL Your work is super important. It's rooted here on the continent, but it has a confidence about its own history that West Africans often lack. We, in West Africa, tend to see ourselves as somehow closer to Europe, and it's partly because we have a colonial relationship, not a settler relationship. The settler, or dominion, relationship is a different one. It has also made us much more vulnerable to an erosion of our own traditions, ways of seeing things, because it's not framed as a colonial relationship. It's framed to be modern, and as progress. There actually isn't that deep pool of resistance here because the British

came, they took some gold and they pretty much left. They didn't stay here. There's no English man who came here to become Ghanaian. It was totally extractive and administrative, and when it became a little bit too challenging, they just buggered off. East Africa and Southern Africa is a different story all together.

KK This leads me to the next question. The Anthropocene Museum research and practice is paving the way for a new institution in the Great Rift Valley, the so-called 'cradle of humankind'. At least that's where we think it's leading us. A place that you highlight where the European settlers came and as you say felt, "I can call this place home, to not only extract resources, but to bring their families here to settle." With our museum making mindset, what would you say is the most critical thing to consider when making an institution in Africa, as you have done with the African Futures Institute [AFI] in Accra, Ghana? Why do you feel it's important to revisit institution building in this age, especially in Africa?

LL The one thing I have come to realise about institutions is that almost no matter what the vision or the mission of the institution is, the administration, that is the substructure, is the same everywhere. It doesn't really matter whether the institute is in Accra, it's in Johannesburg, it's in London.

What the Global North have to their great advantage is two hundred or three hundred years of finessing the relationship between Indigenous culture and administration. If you think about the French colonial enterprise, its administrators were sent to the finest schools. There's a whole culture around becoming a really top-notch administrator. The British

Civil Service, in a sense, is an example of that. This is an administrative culture that rolls on no matter who's in government and that is in the business of both disseminating, controlling and building power. Particular governments come in, they have a take on something, but they're not the real power brokers. It's the subculture that rolls.

We don't have that on this continent. We might not have the long-term translation of Indigenous ways of organising ourselves to fit contemporary organisational structure. It's so basic right down to the relationship of hierarchy. One of the things I've realised since I came back to Ghana is that we are still a deeply feudal culture. And it's not to say that feudality is better or worse than modernity, actually. They're just different. But we never speak about the tension between taking a feudal way of being and trying to mould it into ridiculous things like equity, diversity and inclusivity.

I find, as a sixty-year-old woman, it's conversely harder to get things done here than it was when I was forty because somewhere deep in the psyche, women who are in their sixties, they're grandmothers. They're out to pasture. There's a different dynamic around them. I think people understand a forty-year-old as a go-getter and a twenty-year-old as a hustler. But we never speak about this.

Now my funding comes from overseas and I find myself in Africa defending my EDI policies [equality, diversity and inclusion], which is such an absurd conundrum. We *are* EDI. We don't have to practice or implement it. I've also come to realise that change can't happen without institution building. So, in some ways, in the conceptual chaos that I see here, where every one man is for himself, every little individual, it's almost impossible for us to coalesce and

to have that administrative and organisational power because we haven't done the really difficult work of translating our own ways of being with one another to that culture.

STELLA MUTEGI I think that perspective may be changing to some extent within the continent. I don't know about West Africa or Ghana, but at least in East Africa, we have older women (grandmothers) taking up non-traditional roles that are within that very feudal society that you are talking about. It is not unusual to have these women taking up positions that allow them to be policymakers as well as decision-makers.

About thirty or more years ago in Kenya, the girl child was deemed vulnerable and lacking in opportunities like the boy child. She had many other responsibilities that the boy child did not have and therefore was not able to excel and pursue careers like the boys. There was a concerted effort by both the government and several organisations to give the same opportunity to the girl child in order for her to excel. She was therefore protected, nurtured and championed, and initiatives and laws were put in place to ensure that the girl child thrived.

This has resulted in a society full of women who play at the same level with men if not even to a greater advantage than the man. The traditional feudal way of positioning a woman is no longer at play and the age of that woman is no longer going to be an issue. What you are doing here in Ghana is setting the ground for little African girls to aspire to. To question the norm, to break boundaries, to be equal, to be diverse and to be included in every sphere of society.

LL Thank you. So ... I don't think that my reflections

on our culture answers your question exactly, but I do think that it's time that we start to ask those kinds of questions of what is the form, space, organisation, programme and planning that will accommodate this period of intense translation. I think we have no idea what that is yet.

KK We're at the infancy of realising an institution. Do we need to accept that time and that process, do we need to find ways to bypass that lack? Or do we just need to roll with the motion of things?

LL It's a complex question. I always say that architecture is a profound act of translation: idea-drawing, drawing-model, model-building, building-city. You are constantly doing this. I don't think there's an African alive who doesn't speak more than one language. We are all translators from the cradle. We also translate worlds. Even to be on this continent, you are constantly translating between a so-called Indigenous way of life and a modern. So we have the tools. We understand the tactic and the terrain. I would say, by and large, we don't have the leadership. The leadership is the missing component that can take the emotion, the history, the experience and the longing, and translate that into a thing, whether that's an institute, a museum, a university, a programme or an airport. And I think we are still very much in the middle of trying to figure out, who are those leaders, what gives them the authority.

SM I'm just thinking about that question, "Where are they, and when will they come?" With the various people that I've been talking to here in Ghana, and every time you mention anything to do with development, we all go, "Yes, that's how Africans are." Like the politicians, for instance. There's a special African politician, but it's exactly the same politician you get in Ghana, as you will get in Kenya and Malawi, wherever you are on the continent. And I wonder, at what point that changeover will be? When it will get to architecture in Africa, to the African architect? When will we use the Western architectural education we have received, and translate that into Indigenous African architecture?

LL I think it is happening. And there's a cliched Barack Obama quote: 'We are the change that we seek.' *We are it.* There's no one else. And I think one of the burdens of being an African, is that the minute you lift your head above the parapet, somehow you're now speaking for everybody. The pressure and the expectations that are heaped upon those few people who put their hands up, in some ways, are handicaps. To take architecture as an example, we cannot solve the world. We can do interesting things that act as catalysts for other things to happen, but we don't have the tools and we certainly don't have the answers. What makes me very optimistic now is that actually if you were to say 'African architect' today, there'd be ten or fifteen names popping up. And there's a lot of pressure on those names, I get it. You are speaking for a lot of people who didn't have the opportunity to speak, and nobody ever speaks about what the individual pressure on people is. It's immense. But it's a better situation than it was five years ago, and certainly better than it was ten years ago. And if we "play our cards right," in five years' time, it will be a better situation, still.

I think there's a danger point where you may become so many and so diverse that the outside world, which is quite happy to deal with fifteen or twenty or twenty-five people, suddenly don't want to deal with a hundred. So that game has its own pitfalls and peaks and troughs.

To name something is to segregate it

KK Many museums in the recent colonial past were institutional conduits of extraction and erasure, reinscribing geology effectively on a global scale, as Kathryn Yusoff [professor of inhuman geography at Queen Mary University of London, UK, and author of *A Billion Black Anthropocenes or None* (2018)], also would say.

With the current impetus for structural change in many of these institutions, and that is museums abroad mainly, do you feel there is substantive and sufficient change being made in the right direction as it relates to repatriation of artefacts and providing redress for communities affected? And what do you feel might be the missing link or element in the whole process – is there something we're not getting right?

LL It's a great question. I always think back to around 2005, when I was teaching at the University of Cape Town. We took a group of students to see the Museum of Struggle in Port Elizabeth, by Jo Noero [South African architect]. It was just before it opened, and at that time, there were lots of South African cities that all had an apartheid museum. It was quite a vogue thing. So, the museum was located in the township, which is not typical. It was usually in a suburb. And Noero made the unusual decision to have the workforce that built the museum come from the township. But it was a big struggle because the workers were like, "We lived through apartheid, why are we going to build a museum to it?" There was a lot of tension and problems.

Anyway, we take these students there, we drive there for two days, we go to see the museum, and as we are walking around the museum, I noticed that the signage is in three languages: English, Xhosa and Afrikaans. And the signs in English and Afrikaans, you could understand. Even if you didn't speak Afrikaans, you could translate it: "Museum Entrance, Museum Exit, Museum Shop, Museum Restaurant," whatever. But the Xhosa word every single time was different and sometimes they were long words, sometimes they were short words. So I eventually called a security guard and I asked, "What is that word? What does it mean?" He said, "Oh, it means 'Door that goes this way.' And this means 'Place where you sit down.'" And I said, "Well, what about the word museum? Why isn't it called a museum restaurant?" And then he goes and calls another security guard, and the two of them come over and there's a little chit chat. And then it turns out that there's no word in Xhosa for a museum. So I asked him, "What do you call a place like this building?" They chatted amongst themselves and he said, "This is a building for white people." So I said, "Well, what do you call a building where you go to remember things?" He looked at me and said, "Madam, you don't need a building for that."

SM Because our memory is in our head.

LL Or it's in the landscape, or it's in rituals. I think he found the idea strange that you would have a specific place, which was the place that you would go to, to remember? He couldn't understand the logic in that. You remember the past everywhere, in songs, in recipes.

It's a cliched way to think about it, but it got me thinking for the first time about the relationship between programme and race. You call something a school, a museum, an institute. You name it, but you also secure it. It's, first and foremost, an act of, I would say, segregation. So what happens when you come with a practice that is not about boundary? It's about boundary breaking, understanding that the ancestors are present in the present, understanding that there's a much more fluid relationship between past, present and future. These are really world paradigms. And as architects, we have no idea what the translation of that into form would be.

Architecture either is or it isn't

SM That's really made me think that there's so much in architecture that's very obvious to the Global North, but is so vague in Africa, because there's no … way to define or to translate it. Just like the guards you mention at the Museum of Struggle in South Africa described, there has never been a physical manifestation for a place of remembrance hence the reason they would refer to the museum as a building for white people.

The idea that remembrance in the West manifests as a museum, a physical building, how does remembrance that was historically passed down generations orally manifest in Africa through architecture without borrowing the same idea from the Western set concept? This also is the question to ask for a lot of borrowed Western architecture that doesn't necessarily work the same way because of the culture that we have.

LL The translation is not accurate. To go back to that question of language, you occupy two paradigms simultaneously. And architecture is particularly diffi-

cult because it doesn't sit well in the in-between. Architecture either is or it isn't. So what does one have to do to architecture in order to make it comfortable in that, I don't want to call it an in-between space, it's almost more like a simultaneous space? I realise I'm speaking very esoterically, but when you really get down to it you start to question, "When I draw a line, when I make something out of this material, when I make a placement like this on the earth, what am I actually saying with that act?" I think almost nowhere on this continent do we teach students to question that. What we teach them to do is to make *that* as technically proficient and as close to the copy as it possibly can be. But we very rarely go to the original.

KK I think that's really interesting for us because when we began going into caves, talking to the communities, realising how rich the stories they were telling us were, facts we couldn't find in any books, we began to think, "Okay, we need to compile and record this, and then showcase it outside."

For a long time we thought this process we were employing might be very extractive, where we collect, condense and tell the story and administer it in museums and gallery spaces. However we soon realised that the real logic was seeing that the museum with all its richness and operations within the community setting was always there. It was all happening right before our eyes and we did not initially see it. In a way, we've come full circle now to ask, "Within these territories and, within these spaces of communities, what is the least and the most we should do to retain that authenticity?" But as an architect, our tools are almost inadequate to make it thrive better.

LL In some ways, I disagree because I think actually the tools that architects have are infinite. Hilary Mantel [1952-2022], who's one of my favourite writers, died yesterday. She was asked by the *Financial Times* earlier this month whether she believed in an afterlife. Mantel said she did, but that she couldn't imagine how it could work: "However, the universe isn't limited by what I can imagine," she said.

I would say the same about architects. The ways in which we deploy the tools are increasingly circumscribed. Accreditation, validation, technical proficiency. All of that professional rhetoric, to me, is the same attempt to bound and to classify. But the amazing thing about Africa, it's one of the reasons why I find this continent so optimistic, is that because we've never had any faith in the structures that bind us, we have always resisted, in some way, shape or form. Instinctively, we keep on resisting. So when someone says to you, "Draw it like this," if you're in the right environment, your first question is "Why?", because you can't take anything about history or the world around you for granted.

The flip side of that, and I think this is something that's very problematic here, is that we often equate culture and tradition. We think they're the same thing. Actually, culture is the mechanism by which you change. It's the fuel. Tradition by its very nature is static. Tradition is the way things were done. And it's not that culture doesn't have something to do with tradition, but they're not the same thing.

KK I think the weakness, or the achilles heel, of museums is that very thing: to merge the two and force them in. You see that in so many of the museum institutions, where young people don't feel they have the interest or connection and don't see it as something that's adapting, evolving.

LL Absolutely. There's a really interesting Nigerian group called Looty, they use LIDAR technologies, 3D scanning technology to scan looted artefacts and assign an NFT to it, a non-fungible token. The word Looty was the name given to the Pekingese dog that was given to Queen Victoria in Shanghai. The dog was then brought back to the UK and started the Pekingese breed. So it's a play on the nickname of the dog, but it's also to do with looting artefacts.

So they're essentially building a digital repository [Looty.art], which has value. Actually, it replicates the museum structure, the institutional structure, because museums are all about collections and value and wealth.

They're very interesting. And what I always want to know is, what was the education? That's the question I asked you guys the other night during your lecture at the AFI when you spoke about your research and practice at Cave_bureau. What is the education you went through, the process you went through, that freed you up to think in certain ways? Because that is what we have to replicate. So that somebody doesn't have to go to Westminster or Australia or Yale or wherever. Because in Africa, since our culture has been consistently under attack, we run to tradition as the place to defend ourselves and then lose that possibility to continuously change. But if there's anything I've learned about architecture, it's that it's always changing states, it changes at its very heart. And so we must.

Lesley Lokko OBE is a Ghanaian-Scottish architect, academic and novelist. She is curator of the 18th Venice Biennale of Architecture (2023). Lokko is founder and head of the Graduate School of Architecture (GSA) at the University of Johannesburg, South Africa. Furthermore, she is the author of several books including *White Papers, Black Marks: Race, Culture, Architecture* (UNKNO, 2000).

This conversation took place on the occasion of the Architecture in Africa's International Relations (AAIR) – African State Architecture (ASA) Workshop on 24 September 2022, where Cave_bureau participated as keynote speakers. AAIR is held at the African Futures Institute in Accra, Ghana. The AFI is led and founded by Lesley Lokko.

Waters of Ol Doinyo Nyukie

The Anthropocene Museum 10.0

As a grounding chapter of The Anthropocene Museum, we signal a return back to the Great Rift Valley where it all began, revisiting the first site of our Anthropocene Museum 1.0 on Mount Suswa. The project looks to tackle the current pressures and demands of urbanisation on such a pristine and remote site that has become next in line for the government's plans to exploit the rich resources of geothermal energy, with Kenya being the seventh highest producer in the world.

For this urban research project, we take a decentralised approach, looking outside the city to examine and address the myriad of ways that its anthropogenic pressures are negatively affecting a resilient people, the Maasai, who are struggling to adapt the ingenious ways of living that have sustained them for thousands of years. The Maasai community of Suswa are facing the impacts of 2022 and the worst recorded drought in forty years, with their livelihood of rearing cows and goats decimated and their ability to earn a living drastically affected.

The Anthropocene Museum 10.0 is an architecture and landscape project that looks to support and expand the community's already proactive and resilient approaches to managing their diminishing water supplies through the creation of efficient and sustainable water reservoirs. The project will generate a site-specific design intervention on an outer crater on community conservancy land. It is a project about respect and restorative justice, working closely with the Maasai to co-design solutions that bolster their agency and Indigenous structures of governance, with a view to the flourishing of both human and more-than-human life on the mountain.

Anthropocene Museum 10.0: *Waters of Ol Doinyo Nyukie*, Cave_bureau on field work visiting the Maasai people of Ol Doinyo Nyukie, 2022.

Cave_bureau, *Waters of Ol Doinyo Nyukie* collages. Made for the Maasai people of Ol Doinyo Nyukie, the *Waters of Ol Doinyo Nyukie* is an infrastructure of rainwater reservoirs to mitigate water scarcity during Kenya's harsh, climate change-induced droughts. Upscaling the age old Maasai methods and means of adaptation to an ever changing world.

Cave
bureau

© 2023 Louisiana Museum of Modern Art,
Lars Müller Publishers and the contributors
Edited by Mette Marie Kallehauge and Malou Wedel Bruun
Graphic design: Camilla Jørgensen and Søren Damstedt, Trefold
Editorial assistance: Pernille Gøtze Johansson
Translation from the Danish: Adam King (foreword)
Proofreading: Henry Broome
Cover: © Kabage Karanja

Litho/Print: Narayana Press
ISBN Louisiana Museum of Modern Art: 978-87-93659-65-0
ISBN Lars Müller Publishers: 978-3-03778-731-1
Printed in Denmark 2023

Louisiana Museum of Modern Art
Humlebæk, Denmark
www.louisiana.dk

Lars Müller Publishers
Zürich, Switzerland
www.lars-mueller-publishers.com

Distributed in North America by ARTBOOK / D.A.P.
www.artbook.com

This catalogue is published on the occasion of the exhibition
The Architect's Studio
Cave_bureau – The Anthropocene Museum
Louisiana Museum of Modern Art
29 June – 26 November 2023

Curators: Kjeld Kjeldsen and Mette Marie Kallehauge
Curatorial Coordinator/Registrar: Marianne Ahrensberg
Exhibition Producer and Conservator: Camilla Thorsen Vilslev
Exhibition Architect: Brian Lottenburger
Assistant: Mari Reme Sagedal
Graphic Design: Marie Lübecker

All photos/drawings: © Cave_bureau
Except for: © Khadija Saye: p. 14-15, 148; © Kabage Karanja: p. 20-21
(bottom), 59, 78, 79, 189, 209; © Densu Moseti: p. 38-41, 56-57, 98, 85,
88 (bottom), 89, 125, 127, 129, 206; © History, World & People: p. 58;
© Museum of London: p. 62; © G. F. Bosworth: p. 64; © Carole Raddato:
p. 65; © Emma Lynch/BBC: p. 67; © Shermozle (Licenced by Creative
Commons): p. 68; © Francesco Galli: p. 72-75, 78, 80-81; © Nigel
Pavitt, *Kenya: A Country in the Making 1880-1940* (W. W. Norton &
Company, 2008): p. 86, 127; © Boniface Mwangi: p. 87; © David Stanley
(Licenced by Creative Commons): p. 88 (top); © Open Government
License, The National Archive: p. 128 (top); © Gualtiero Jacopetti and
Franco Prosperi / AnotherWorld Entertainment: p. 128 (bottom);
© The GoDown Arts Centre: p. 130-131, 134-135 (top); © Paul Munene:
p. 132-133; © James Muriuki: p. 134-135 (bottom); © Joseph Conteh:
p. 29, 144-145; © Google Earth: p. 146; © Kenya Survey Map: p. 147;
© Thornton White, L. Silberman, P.R. Anderson, Nairobi Master Plan
for a Colonial Capital, His Majesty's Stationery Office, 1948: p.150;
© Bernard Safran: p. 151; © Simon Weyhe: p. 155; © Jack Young: p. 155,
160; © Phil Ayres: p. 156-157; © Johan Henrik Reeh: p. 158-159; © Brad
Simpson: p. 162.

All images in this catalogue are intended to be credited as required.
We reserve the right for possible crediting errors.

The exhibition is supported by:

Sponsor of Louisiana's architectural exhibitions